julie's
EATS & TREATS

COOKBOOK

JULIE EVINK

Acknowledgments

TO MY READERS: A huge thank-you to my amazing, supportive blog readers who have been there throughout the years as I found my groove developing recipes. This cookbook wouldn't be possible without you, and I thank you from the bottom of my heart.

TO JASON: I love you. You are my rock, my biggest cheerleader, and I'm so unbelievably lucky to do this life with you. Thank you for always encouraging me to do the scary things, picking up the pieces if they don't pan out, and ordering pizza when a recipe goes straight into the garbage. I could not have done any of this without you by my side.

TO KINZEE, RYLIN, AND KOERT: You three are my everything. Being your parent is one of the biggest blessings on earth. Thank you for always letting me try new recipes on you, pausing for photos before you eat, and always rating them with only the most honest feelings possible. There's no shortage of getting your opinions on things!

TO MY PARENTS: Mom and Dad, I don't even know where to start. You have blessed me so much in life. You gave me the room to grow, make mistakes, and dream big, knowing I had a safety net. Mom, those family dinners you made every single night are the reason I do what I do. I know at the time you didn't realize the influence they would have on my life, so thank you for showing up each night. Dad, your work ethic showed me that anything is possible in life if you give it your all—which you do to this day. I will forever be your little girl. Thank you for instilling your values in me so I could achieve my dreams. Mom and Dad, I hope you know just how much I appreciate everything you've done for me.

TO MY BROTHERS: Thanks for giving me the thick skin early on in life to prepare for my future of Internet trolls, but always being there to cheer me on. To Brent, for giving me a hug just when I need it, to this day. To Ryan, I can't wait to sign this cookbook and deliver it to you with a smile on my face. Love you guys!

TO THE REST OF MY FAMILY: I have been truly blessed in the family department, from in-laws to nieces, nephews, aunts, uncles, and cousins. Many of you have sampled recipes, asked me questions, and just plain old supported me. Thanks for getting excited about this crazy career with me!

TO MY DEAR FRIENDS: Our home is always open to you, there's always food in the fridge and pantry (or snack room, as my kids call it!), and your kids are always loved like our own in our home. You have all been so supportive in this adventure. I appreciate each and every one of you. You will never understand how much your support has meant to me over the years.

Dedication

To my family, friends, and readers for encouraging me to make my dream of publishing a cookbook a reality. Thank you for allowing me to do what I love every day. Without you this book would have never been possible!

ACKNOWLEDGMENTS // 2

INTRODUCTION // 9

IN THE KITCHEN WITH JULIE // 12

MUFFINS AND BREADS // 43

Banana Chocolate Chip Muffins // 44

Blueberry Muffins // 47

Cruffins // 48

Banana Bread // 51

Pumpkin Bread // 52

Cheesy Garlic Bread Loaf // 55

Beer Bread // 56

Cheddar Biscuits // 59

Texas Roadhouse Rolls // 60

BREAKFASTS // 19

Berry Baked Oatmeal // 20

Fluffy Pancakes // 23

Waffles // 24

French Toast // 27

Breakfast Crescent Ring // 28

Ham and Cheese Egg Muffins // 31

Breakfast Enchiladas // 32

Hash Brown Breakfast Casserole // 35

Biscuit and Gravy Breakfast Casserole // 36

Caramel Pull-Aparts // 39

Easy Cinnamon Rolls // 40

Contents

SOUPS AND STEWS // 95

Broccoli Cheese Soup // 96
Chicken and Rice Soup // 99
Creamy Chicken Noodle Soup // 100
Chicken and Wild Rice Soup // 103
Hamburger Soup // 104
Sausage and Potato Soup // 107
Lasagna Soup // 108
Chili // 111
Slow Cooker White Chicken Chili // 112
Slow Cooker Enchilada Soup // 115
Slow Cooker Zuppa Toscana // 116
Slow Cooker Beef Stew // 119

SALADS AND SIDES // 63

Tossed Salad with Italian Dressing // 64
Pea Salad // 67
Potato Salad // 68
Macaroni Salad // 71
Dorito Taco Salad // 72
Oreo Fluff // 75
Strawberry Pretzel Salad // 76
Fried Rice // 79
Spanish Rice // 80
Cheesy Garlic-Butter Pasta // 83
Roasted Sweet Potatoes // 84
Cheesy Bacon Ranch Potatoes // 87
Funeral Potatoes // 88
Oven-Roasted Vegetables // 91
Bacon-Wrapped Green Beans // 92

Contents

DINNERS // 121

Chicken

Baked Chicken Drumsticks // 122

Baked Chicken Thighs // 125

Baked Chicken Wings // 126

Baked Sweet and Sour Chicken // 129

Honey Sesame Chicken // 130

Chicken Fried Rice // 133

Sheet Pan Chicken Fajitas // 134

Creamy Chicken Enchiladas // 137

Chicken Tetrazzini // 138

Chicken Alfredo Bake // 141

Slow Cooker Bacon Ranch Chicken Sandwiches // 142

Slow Cooker Italian Chicken // 145

One-Pot Cajun Chicken Pasta // 146

Beef

Baked Spaghetti // 149

Homemade Hamburger Helper // 150

Zucchini Hamburger Skillet // 153

Slow Cooker Hamburger and Wild Rice Casserole // 154

Mini Meatloaves // 157

Totchos // 158

Baked Tacos // 161

Beef Enchiladas // 162

One-Pot Taco Pasta // 165

One-Pot Burrito Bowl // 166

Taco Pie // 169

Hamburger Stroganoff // 170

Stuffed Pepper Casserole // 173

Baked Meatballs in Marinara Sauce // 174

Beef and Broccoli // 177

Lasagna // 178

Garlic-Butter Steak and Potatoes // 181

Sheet Pan Steak, Potatoes, and Asparagus // 182

Slow Cooker French Dip Sandwiches // 185

Slow Cooker Mississippi Pot Roast // 186

Pork

Stuffed Zucchini Boats // 189

Pizza Sliders // 190

One-Pot Pizza Pasta // 193

Ham and Potato Casserole // 194

Parmesan-Crusted Pork Chops // 197

Seafood

Parmesan-Crusted Tilapia // 198

Shrimp Boil // 201

Shrimp Pasta // 202

DESSERTS // 205

Fudge Sauce // 206

Oreo Ice Cream Dessert // 209

Buster Bar Dessert // 210

The Best Rice Krispie Treats // 213

No-Bake Cheesecake // 214

Lemon Bundt Cake // 217

Strawberry Poke Cake // 218

Oreo Poke Cake // 221

Strawberry Crisp // 222

Apple Crisp // 225

Strawberry Pie // 226

Fruit Pizza // 229

Banana Bars // 230

Pumpkin Bars // 233

Peanut Butter Cereal Bars // 234

Salted Nut Roll Bars // 237

Knock You Naked Bars // 238

Monster Cookie Bars // 241

Oatmeal Cookies // 242

Chocolate Chip Cookies // 245

Pumpkin Snickerdoodle Cookies // 246

Reese's Pieces Peanut Butter Cookies // 249

Chocolate Cherry Brownies // 250

INDEX 252

Introduction

Hi, I'm Julie! I like to call myself the Midwestern mom next door. You'll most likely find me in slippers, cozy clothes, sipping a coffee while reading. You know you're a true friend when I call you my "sweatpants" friend, a.k.a. I'm not changing out of my sweats or cleaning my house for you! If you're reading this book, it's safe to say you are that kind of friend.

Since you are my sweatpants friend, it's very likely that when you come over, I'm going to make you a treat, because food is my love language. That's how I show my family and friends just how much I love them.

I truly believe in making delicious food that anyone can cook using pantry staple ingredients. Don't worry—the food I make is still full of flavor and I sneak in as many fresh ingredients as possible.

Now, just because I'm a food blogger doesn't mean I'm making you a five-course meal. You'll often find me chasing after three kids and a husband. There are concerts, ball games, playdates, and more. I know how hard it is to make a dinner the entire family will eat and get it on the table. Plus, when you live in a town of 5,000 people in Midwest Minnesota that has one grocery store, the ingredients in your recipes must be simple and relatively easy to find, so I will not send you to five grocery stores to find an ingredient. Nope, never—because we don't have time for that!

Know that I have tested all these recipes multiple times on my family and they approve of them. That's saying a lot, if you know what I mean!

Why is this so important to me? I grew up on a farm in Midwest Minnesota and "supper" was served at 6:30 p.m. every single night, like clockwork. We put everything down and gathered for a meal. Dad even quit farming most of the time!

Having this experience as a child made me firmly believe in family meals as often as possible. It's a time to put the world aside and have family time, reflect on what the day brought and what tomorrow will bring. My goal is to give you recipes that let you do this, while not losing your mind. Think 30-minute meals, simple ingredients, and pantry staples, so you can make dinner, clean up, and be on to the next activity.

Don't worry, I snuck lots of treats into this cookbook, too. If you know me, you know that sweets are my downfall. Plus, there are some epic breakfast recipes. A few even double as "brinner," which is breakfast for dinner. That's always a hit at our house!

I hope that as you sit down with these recipes, you feel the love through the pages and they help your life become just a little bit more manageable. That is always my goal. I'm so thankful that I get to share my favorite food with you through this cookbook. I hope you jump right in and that these recipes quickly become your family's favorites and the ones you pass along to friends and down the generations.

In the Kitchen with Julie

A MEAL PLAN

I am the biggest advocate of making a meal plan for the week. It takes the stress out of mealtimes and helps make preparing dinner approachable. Here's why I love a weekly meal plan.

SAVES TIME: Make a grocery list and then just one trip to the grocery store at the beginning of the week for all your meals. Better yet, do a grocery pickup. It also saves you from standing in the kitchen at dinnertime wondering what to make, or letting time tick by while you search for a recipe each night.

SAVES STRESS: I'm a big-time fan of having a plan in life. Now, it might not always go perfectly, but at least I feel prepared. When I get to dinnertime and know I have a recipe and the ingredients ready to go, it makes it a lot less stressful than when I'm wandering around my kitchen, searching the Internet, or making a last-minute trip to the store.

SAVES MONEY: Shop for the ingredients you need and only those. Make sure when you write down your grocery list that you check your pantry and refrigerator for ingredients you already have on hand, so you don't buy them again. Or if you know you have food that needs to be eaten, create your meal plan around what you have so it doesn't go to waste. To save a little extra, use the weekly grocery ads to plan your meals around what's on sale.

AVOIDS THE RUT: You know the rut: the meals you make over and over again and pretty soon you don't want to look at them anymore! Planning ahead gives you time to look for a new recipe or ingredients you might want to try.

I hope this book helps you win in the kitchen again!

KIDS IN THE KITCHEN

I sure wish I could give you the magic button that gets your children to eat everything you make. Unfortunately, I'm not a magician! But I might have some helpful tips I've figured out over my few short years of motherhood.

My biggest thing is I'm not my children's personal chef. I refuse to make five different meals every time we sit down to eat. That's exhausting, it's not fun, and it's frustrating for everyone.

We always have our children try the things we make. Just one bite if it's something new. If they decide they don't like it, then we roll with it. Sometimes you have to pick your battles—am I right?

What do we do when they don't like something? They are more than welcome to make toast, cereal, mac and cheese, grab some leftovers, whatever. But as soon as they are old enough, they have to make it themselves. Remember, I'm not a personal chef.

I figure I'm encouraging them to try new things and teaching them a little independence by learning how to make themselves meals. Usually they eat whatever I make, because it's easier.

We also are big fans of getting our kids in the kitchen when they are young to start learning the basics of how to cook and bake. When they are young it's simple things, but their curiosity at that age is so much fun. Plus they are more likely to try new things if they

are making them. They may mix something for 30 seconds and drift away, but little by little those lessons add up. And as they grow they get more confident and it's so much fun to watch!

Plus, when they are older and have these skills, encourage them to use them and make you dinner one night a week! Having patience and encouraging them in the kitchen when they are younger—because, once again, real life sometimes is a challenge—can have huge benefits later.

So, what this boils down to is encourage your children in the kitchen by having them help out in baking and cooking, and trying new foods, but give them grace and roll with the punches as much as possible.

MY 10 FAVORITE KITCHEN TOOLS

✱ **My slow cooker** There are always fancy new kitchen gadgets coming out, but I always go straight back to my slow cooker. It gets me through so many days. It is the number one thing on my list forever and always.

✱ **My sharp knives** I cannot tell you how much a good set of knives changes your life! It makes cooking so much more enjoyable. Learn how to sharpen them, wash them by hand, and treat them like you love them.

✱ **My kid-safe knives** We gave our kids "safe" knives when they were super young and they loved them. It helped them feel useful in the kitchen when I was chopping things up, and yet I knew they wouldn't lose their fingers!

✱ **My apron and kids' aprons** I can't tell you how many times I've ruined clothes due to grease splatters. Grab yourself a cute apron, and get matching aprons for the kids. It makes getting in the kitchen and going to work a lot more fun when you feel cute! I figure there's a reason my grandma always wore her apron, and I'm going to take one from her book.

✱ **My cast-iron Dutch oven** This is a tool I got only a few years ago, and I reach for it multiple times a week. It's something I didn't think I needed, but now will never go without. It's such a big help with soups and one-pot meals!

✱ **My stand mixer** Can you believe my mom's sat in a corner in the kitchen when I was growing up? Every time I make cookies I think of that! Using a hand mixer for a big batch of cookies? Nope, get the stand mixer. Bread? Get the stand mixer. Cinnamon roll dough? Get the stand mixer. Invest in one and you'll be using it for years and years to come.

✳ **My box grater** You'll see in many of my recipes I note to grab a block of cheese and grate it. If you want that to-die-for melty cheese, get a box grater and grate your own cheese. It makes such a difference, and is worth the extra couple of minutes it takes.

✳ **My cookie scoop** I remember scooping cookies with a spoon growing up, and as soon as I found out there were cookie scoops, I was like, *Come again?* Get one—you won't regret it! You'll have the perfect size cookies every single time.

✳ **My nonstick skillet** I think sometimes nonstick skillets get a bad rap, but I forever and always will make sure I have a nice one in my kitchen. You can't beat it for making eggs, browning meat, and a lot more.

✳ **My stool for the kids** Remember how I said to get them in the kitchen? Having a tall stool helps so much so they can be at the perfect level to help safely and easily. It doesn't have to be anything fancy—just get one!

GROCERY LIST

Remember Mom running around with her pad of paper and pen at the grocery store, crossing things off as she added them to the cart? I sure do!

I'm going to take one from Mom's book and tell you to make a grocery list. We lived on the farm and were ten miles from town, so if we didn't have something she needed it meant a call to the neighbors down the road to see if they did, not another trip to town.

Once again, take some stress out of life by making a list, so you can make one grocery shopping trip a week instead of several. I know, I know, things come up and life happens, but trying to do this makes things a lot less stressful and saves *time*—and *money* too, because we all know we grab a few extra things each trip!

✳ **How do you make a list?** Go old school with a pad of paper in the kitchen or stuck on the refrigerator, if that works; or go high tech and get an app on your phone.

I love having my smart device, Alexa, in my kitchen. I connect my shopping list to it, and I have trained my children and husband (yes, it took a while!) to tell Alexa to put things on the list as we run out. It's absolutely life-changing. They know if it's not on the list, Mom doesn't buy it!

I cannot tell you how much having a simple grocery list will help with stress management and streamline your life.

MY 10 FAVORITE PANTRY STAPLES

* **Vanilla extract**   Always splurge and get pure vanilla extract. Its rich flavor will level up your baking game.

* **Block cheese**   I know it's so handy to grab the bag of shredded cheese, but grating it yourself will always result in a better melt. It is so worth the extra few minutes of prep time.

* **Fresh spices and baking leaveners**   Did you know they expire? The spices lose their potency, and your baking won't give you the results you want with old leaveners. Check them once a year. I always do it at Christmas when I do my Christmas baking—super easy time to remember!

* **Rice**   Seems boring, right? I always have a bag of rice, often several different kinds, in my pantry because it's an easy side dish and my kids love it. Plus it's cheap.

* **Frozen chopped onions**   Stock your freezer with them. I found these, and my life has been changed! Yes, there might be more flavor in fresh, so if that's your thing keep the fresh. But not crying over chopping onions? I'm here for it.

* **Pasta**   I always have a ton of different types of pasta. It makes meals more fun, it's cheap, and it's a great base. Plus, hello buttered noodles and spaghetti, because my kids will always eat that!

* **Coffee**   Mom (and Dad) gotta survive somehow! Fresh beans that you grind are truly the best, but you'll find me with my K-cups for convenience.

* **Evaporated milk**   This is my hack for creamy soups. I love using evaporated milk instead of heavy cream because I never have that in my refrigerator.

* **Canned chicken**   I never thought I'd write this, but I've embraced it. I was once too good for it, but the truth is it's a great option when recipes call for shredded chicken. I use it in soups, quesadillas, casseroles, and similar dishes.

* **Frozen ground beef**   I grew up on a farm and our freezer was always stocked with beef. This has not changed. Having a supply of ground beef, or meat of any kind in the freezer is so handy. Watch for sales, or order a quarter of a cow from the local butcher.

Shop Julie's faves!

Fluffy Pancakes, page 23

Breakfasts

Berry Baked Oatmeal // 20

Fluffy Pancakes // 23

Waffles // 24

French Toast // 27

Breakfast Crescent Ring // 28

Ham and Cheese Egg Muffins // 31

Breakfast Enchiladas // 32

Hash Brown Breakfast Casserole // 35

Biscuit and Gravy Breakfast Casserole // 36

Caramel Pull-Aparts // 39

Easy Cinnamon Rolls // 40

SERVES 6

PREP TIME: 15 MINS
COOK TIME: 40 MINS
TOTAL TIME: 55 MINS

Berry BAKED OATMEAL

This delicious baked oatmeal is loaded with fresh berries. It's a quick and easy make-ahead breakfast that is also healthy. I used strawberries, blueberries, and raspberries, but choose whatever you like.

INGREDIENTS

- Nonstick cooking spray
- 3 cups old-fashioned rolled oats
- 1½ teaspoons baking powder
- ½ teaspoon salt
- 3 cups fresh berries, larger berries chopped or sliced
- 2 eggs, lightly beaten
- 2½ cups milk, plus more for serving
- ½ cup pure maple syrup
- 3 Tablespoons melted unsalted butter or coconut oil
- 2 teaspoons vanilla extract

INSTRUCTIONS

1. Preheat the oven to 350 degrees Fahrenheit. Spray a 2½- or 3-quart baking dish with nonstick cooking spray.

2. In a large bowl, combine the oats, baking powder, and salt. Place half the oat mixture in the baking dish, top with half the berries, and then with the remaining oat mixture.

3. In a large bowl, whisk together the eggs, milk, maple syrup, butter or coconut oil, and vanilla. Pour over the oats. Top that with the remaining berries. Gently shake the baking dish back and forth and from side to side to enable the egg mixture to get down into the oats.

4. Bake uncovered for 35 to 40 minutes, until the oats are tender and the mixture is set.

5. Serve immediately with a splash of milk, or cool, then cover and refrigerate in individual portions to reheat later.

JULIE'S *Notes*

You can also use frozen berries, but color from them might bleed into the oatmeal a little bit.

Scan for more tips!

Fluffy PANCAKES

These perfect light and fluffy pancakes melt in your mouth. They are out-of-this world amazing and are made with pantry staples.

12 PANCAKES

PREP TIME: 10 MINS

COOK TIME: 15 MINS

TOTAL TIME: 25 MINS

INGREDIENTS

- 1½ cups all-purpose flour
- 2 Tablespoons white granulated sugar
- 1 Tablespoon baking powder
- ¾ teaspoon salt
- 1 egg
- 1¼ cups milk, divided
- 2 Tablespoons salted butter, melted, plus about 2 Tablespoons for the pan

INSTRUCTIONS

1. Sift the flour, sugar, baking powder, and salt in a large bowl.
2. In another bowl, beat the egg until it's light and fluffy. Add 1 cup of the milk and the melted butter and stir until combined; some lumps are fine.
3. Add the wet ingredients to the dry ingredients and mix until moistened. At this point if the batter is too thick, add the remaining ¼ cup of milk a little at a time until you reach the consistency you want.
4. Heat a large griddle or nonstick skillet over medium-low heat. Melt about ½ Tablespoon of the butter in the skillet. Ladle the batter (about ¼ cup of batter for each pancake) into the skillet, making three or four pancakes. Cook the pancakes until bubbles form on top, about 2 minutes. Flip and brown the other side, about 2 minutes more.
5. Wipe any excess butter from the skillet with paper towels. Repeat with the remaining butter and batter.

JULIE'S Notes

MIX-IN IDEAS: *1 cup fresh blueberries, 1 cup semi-sweet chocolate chips, 1 cup sliced fresh strawberries, and cheddar cheese, too, for a fun twist.*

Scan for more tips!

BREAKFASTS 23

SERVES 4

PREP TIME: 10 MINS

COOK TIME: 10 MINS

TOTAL TIME: 20 MINS

WAFFLES

Wow! That's all I can say about these perfect waffles. They are crispy on the outside and fluffy on the inside, plus they melt in your mouth! When we tested this recipe, every single one of us was raving and asking for seconds.

INGREDIENTS

2 cups all-purpose flour

2 Tablespoons white granulated sugar

1 Tablespoon baking powder

¾ teaspoon salt

2 eggs

1⅔ cups milk

6 Tablespoons melted unsalted butter or vegetable oil, plus more for greasing the waffle iron

2 teaspoons vanilla extract

INSTRUCTIONS

1. Preheat a waffle iron according to the manufacturer's directions (or to 400 degrees Fahrenheit if your waffle maker has a temperature gauge).

2. Whisk the flour, sugar, baking powder, and salt in a large bowl to combine. In a medium bowl, mix the eggs, milk, butter or vegetable oil, and vanilla. Mix the wet ingredients into the dry ingredients until combined.

3. Grease the waffle iron, then drop the batter by large spoonfuls onto the waffle iron until most of the wells are covered. Close the lid and cook for 3 to 5 minutes, until the waffles are golden brown. Repeat with the rest of the batter.

JULIE'S Notes

If you're making the waffles in batches, preheat the oven to 225 degrees Fahrenheit and place a baking pan in the oven. Place the cooked waffles in the baking pan to stay warm while you cook the remaining waffles.

French TOAST

SERVES 5

PREP TIME: 10 MINS
COOK TIME: 8 MINS
TOTAL TIME: 18 MINS

This classic homemade French toast is made with hearty bread that is dunked in a custard batter and cooked until golden brown and crispy. Top with whipped cream, fresh berries, and your favorite syrup.

INGREDIENTS

- 4 eggs
- ¾ cup whole milk
- 2 teaspoons vanilla extract
- 1 Tablespoon white granulated sugar
- 1½ teaspoons ground cinnamon
- 10 thick slices bread
- Unsalted butter for the griddle
- Optional toppings: Whipped cream, fresh berries, and syrup

INSTRUCTIONS

1. Preheat a nonstick griddle to 350 degrees Fahrenheit. You can also use a large nonstick skillet over medium-low heat.

2. In a large, shallow dish (I like to use a pie plate), whisk together the eggs, milk, vanilla, sugar, and cinnamon.

3. Dip the bread slices, one at a time, into the egg mixture, dredging and turning them so they are coated on both sides.

4. Put a pat of butter on the griddle and let it melt and bubble. Place about five slices on the hot greased griddle and cook until golden brown on the bottom, about 2 minutes. Flip over and cook the other side until golden brown, about 2 minutes longer. Repeat to cook all the bread slices.

5. Remove to a plate and keep warm, or serve immediately with your favorite toppings.

JULIE'S Notes

If you want to keep the French toast warm while you cook the rest, transfer them to a baking sheet and keep in a warm oven (about 200 degrees Fahrenheit) until you finish cooking.

Scan for more tips!

BREAKFASTS 27

SERVES 8

PREP TIME: 20 MINS
COOK TIME: 20 MINS
TOTAL TIME: 40 MINS

Breakfast CRESCENT RING

This fun pastry ring (made with refrigerator crescent dough) is filled with cheese, bacon, and eggs, for the ultimate way to start the day.

INGREDIENTS

- 4 eggs, lightly beaten
- ⅓ cup milk
- ½ teaspoon salt
- ¼ teaspoon ground black pepper
- 2 (8-ounce) tubes refrigerated crescent roll dough
- 1 cup shredded cheddar cheese
- 4 slices bacon, cooked and crumbled

INSTRUCTIONS

1. Preheat the oven to 375 degrees Fahrenheit.

2. In a large bowl, combine the eggs, milk, salt, and pepper and whisk until combined. Heat a medium ungreased skillet over medium heat. Add the egg mixture and scramble until cooked through.

3. Unroll the crescent roll dough and separate into triangles. Arrange the triangles on a 14-inch ungreased pizza pan with the points draped outside the rim of the pan and the wide sides overlapping at the center, leaving a 4-inch opening in the center. Press on the overlapping edges of the dough to seal.

4. Spoon the scrambled eggs over the wide part of the dough ring. Sprinkle the cheese over the eggs and top with the crumbled bacon. Fold the pointed ends of the triangles over the filling, tucking the points under the dough to form a pastry ring with some of the filling visible.

5. Bake for 12 to 15 minutes, until the dough is golden brown. Remove from the oven and let cool for 5 minutes, then slice and serve immediately.

Scan for more tips!

HAM AND CHEESE EGG *Muffins*

Light, fluffy egg muffins with cheese and ham make an easy weekday breakfast. They are also a great option to make ahead for a grab-and-go breakfast.

PREP TIME: 10 MINS
COOK TIME: 25 MINS
TOTAL TIME: 35 MINS

12 MUFFINS

INGREDIENTS

- Nonstick cooking spray
- 12 eggs
- ½ cup milk
- ½ teaspoon salt
- ¼ teaspoon ground black pepper
- ½ cup shredded cheddar cheese
- ½ cup diced ham
- Optional garnish: Chopped chives

INSTRUCTIONS

1. Preheat the oven to 350 degrees Fahrenheit. Spray a 12-cup muffin pan with nonstick cooking spray.
2. In a large bowl, whisk together the eggs, milk, salt, and pepper. Stir in the cheese and ham. Pour the mixture into the 12 prepared muffin cups.
3. Bake for 25 minutes, or until the muffins are set in the middle.

JULIE'S *Notes*

MIX-IN IDEAS: You can use either frozen spinach that has been thawed and the water squeezed out, or fresh spinach that has been cooked. Or try diced tomatoes, finely diced fresh mushrooms, bell peppers, or onions. For protein, cooked ground chicken, ground turkey, ground sausage, chorizo, or crumbled bacon are all great choices.

I recommend using a silicone muffin pan set on a baking sheet for easy release and cleanup.

Store any leftovers in an airtight container in the refrigerator for up to 4 days. To freeze, cool completely, then wrap individually in plastic wrap and place in an airtight container or freezer-safe ziplock bag.

Scan for more tips!

BREAKFASTS 31

8 ENCHILADAS

PREP TIME: 15 MINS
COOK TIME: 45 MINS
TOTAL TIME: 1 HR

Breakfast ENCHILADAS

This is one of my go-to overnight breakfast casseroles. Tortillas that are stuffed with sausage, cheese, and bacon bits, then covered with eggs and baked, are such a fun twist on your traditional breakfast casserole.

INGREDIENTS

Nonstick cooking spray

1 pound ground sausage

2 cups shredded cheddar cheese, divided

1 (3-ounce) package real bacon bits (not the crunchy bits in a jar, but the bacon pieces in a bag), divided

8 (8-inch) flour tortillas

6 eggs

2 cups half-and-half

1 Tablespoon all-purpose flour

½ teaspoon salt

Optional garnish: Sliced green onions

INSTRUCTIONS

1. Spray a 9-x-13-inch baking dish with nonstick cooking spray.

2. In a large skillet, brown the sausage over medium-high heat until it's cooked through, 5 to 7 minutes. Drain off the grease.

3. In a large bowl, stir together the cooked sausage, 1 cup of the cheese, and half the bacon bits. Spoon some of the mixture down the center of one tortilla. Roll it up and place seam side down in the baking dish. Repeat until all eight tortillas are filled.

4. In another large bowl, beat the eggs, half-and-half, flour, and salt. Pour over the tortillas in the baking dish. You can bake the casserole immediately, or cover the dish and refrigerate overnight.

5. When you're ready to bake, preheat the oven to 350 degrees Fahrenheit. Uncover the dish and sprinkle the remaining 1 cup cheese over the tortillas. Sprinkle the rest of the bacon bits over the cheese.

6. Cover with aluminum foil and bake for 35 minutes. Uncover and bake for 10 minutes longer, or until the eggs are set and the cheese is melted.

JULIE'S Notes

You can prep this casserole, freeze it, and then thaw in the refrigerator for about 24 hours. Bake in preheated oven according to directions.

Scan for more tips!

HASH BROWN
Breakfast CASSEROLE

Using frozen hash brown patties makes for a quick and easy breakfast casserole that is perfect for feeding a crowd. You can prepare it the night before to save time in the morning.

SERVES 12

PREP TIME: 15 MINS

COOK TIME: 1 HR

TOTAL TIME: 1 HR 15 MINS

INGREDIENTS

Nonstick cooking spray

7 frozen hash brown patties

1 pound diced ham

2 cups shredded cheddar cheese

10 eggs

½ cup milk

¼ cup sour cream

¼ teaspoon garlic powder

¼ teaspoon onion powder

¼ teaspoon salt

¼ teaspoon ground black pepper

INSTRUCTIONS
---

1. Preheat the oven to 350 degrees Fahrenheit. Spray a 9-x-13-inch baking dish with nonstick cooking spray.

2. Arrange the frozen hash brown patties on the bottom of the baking dish in one layer. Spread the ham over the hash browns and top with shredded cheese.

3. In a large bowl, whisk together the eggs, milk, sour cream, garlic powder, onion powder, salt, and pepper. Pour the egg mixture over the casserole and cover with aluminum foil.

4. Bake for 30 minutes. Uncover and bake for an additional 30 minutes, or until the eggs are set.

JULIE'S *Notes*

You can use 1 pound of cooked sausage meat or 1 pound of cooked bacon to replace the diced ham, or a mixture of both.

You can prep this casserole, freeze it, and then thaw in the refrigerator for about 24 hours. Bake in preheated oven according to directions.

SERVES 8

PREP TIME: 25 MINS
COOK TIME: 50 MINS
CHILL TIME: 4 HRS
TOTAL TIME: 5 HRS 15 MINS

BISCUIT AND GRAVY
Breakfast CASSEROLE

Biscuits with sausage, eggs, and cheese, topped with gravy: What could be better? I've made it into an overnight casserole to make it even easier.

INGREDIENTS

- Nonstick cooking spray
- 1 pound ground pork sausage
- 1 (16.3-ounce) tube Homestyle Buttermilk Pillsbury Grands biscuits
- 1 cup shredded cheddar cheese
- 8 eggs
- 2¼ cups milk, divided
- 1 teaspoon salt, divided
- 1 teaspoon ground black pepper, divided
- Dash of cayenne pepper
- 5 Tablespoons salted butter
- 5 Tablespoons all-purpose flour

INSTRUCTIONS

1. Spray a 9-x-13-inch baking pan with nonstick cooking spray.
2. In a large skillet, brown the sausage over medium-high heat until cooked through, 5 to 7 minutes. Drain off the grease.
3. Cut the biscuits into 1-inch pieces and use to line the bottom of the baking pan. Layer the cooked sausage over the biscuit pieces. Spread the cheese over the sausage.
4. In a large bowl, whisk together the eggs, ¾ cup of the milk, ½ teaspoon of the salt, ½ teaspoon of the black pepper, and a dash of cayenne pepper. Pour the egg mixture over the biscuits. Cover with aluminum foil and refrigerate for at least 4 hours or overnight.
5. Make the gravy the same day: Melt the butter in a medium saucepan. Whisk in the flour until you have a paste, then whisk in the remaining ½ teaspoon salt and the remaining ½ teaspoon black pepper. With the heat on low, gradually whisk in the remaining 1½ cups milk and stir constantly until the mixture becomes thick and gravy-like. Set aside to cool, then place the gravy in a covered container and refrigerate until needed.
6. In the morning, preheat the oven to 350 degrees Fahrenheit.
7. Warm the gravy and pour it over the casserole, covering with aluminum foil. Bake for 35 minutes. Uncover and bake for 10 to 15 more minutes, until the eggs are thoroughly cooked and the cheese starts to turn golden brown.

Scan for more tips!

SERVES 8

Caramel **PULL-APARTS**

These sweet pull-aparts, a recipe from my late mother-in-law, continue to be a most-requested breakfast in my family. The bite-size biscuits are loaded with an ooey gooey caramel sauce made from—surprise!—ice cream.

PREP TIME: 10 MINS

COOK TIME: 18 MINS

TOTAL TIME: 28 MINS

INGREDIENTS

- Nonstick cooking spray
- 3 (7.5-ounce) tubes refrigerated biscuit dough, separated and cut into quarters
- 2 teaspoons ground cinnamon
- ½ cup unsalted butter
- 1 cup vanilla ice cream
- 1 cup packed brown sugar

INSTRUCTIONS

1. Preheat the oven to 375 degrees Fahrenheit. Spray a 9-x-13-inch baking pan with nonstick cooking spray. Arrange the biscuit quarters in the pan and sprinkle with the cinnamon.

2. In a small saucepan, melt the butter, ice cream, and brown sugar, stir to combine, and bring to a boil. Pour over the biscuits.

3. Bake for 18 minutes, until the biscuits are golden brown and cooked through.

4. Cool for 5 minutes in the pan. Then flip the pan over onto a serving platter and serve.

Scan for more tips!

BREAKFASTS 39

12 ROLLS

PREP TIME: 20 MINS

RISE TIME: 1 HR

COOK TIME: 25 MIN

TOTAL TIME: 1 HR 45 MINS

Easy CINNAMON ROLLS

These tender, light, and flaky rolls with a delicious cream cheese frosting on top are a snap to make. If you are nervous about making cinnamon rolls, this is the recipe for you.

INGREDIENTS

DOUGH
- 1 cup whole milk
- ¼ cup white granulated sugar
- 1 (¼-ounce) package (2¼ teaspoons) active dry yeast
- ¼ cup unsalted butter, melted and slightly cooled
- 1 egg, room temperature
- 1 teaspoon vanilla extract
- ½ teaspoon salt
- 3½ cups all-purpose flour, plus more for rolling

CREAM CHEESE FROSTING
- ¼ cup unsalted butter, softened
- 4 ounces cream cheese, softened
- 1½ cups powdered sugar
- 1 teaspoon vanilla extract
- Pinch of salt

FILLING
- ½ cup unsalted butter, softened (see Julie's Notes)
- ½ cup packed brown sugar
- ½ cup white granulated sugar
- 2 Tablespoons ground cinnamon
- 1 teaspoon vanilla extract
- ¼ to ½ cup heavy cream, room temperature

INSTRUCTIONS

1. Line a 9-x-13-inch baking dish with parchment paper.

2. Start the dough: In a large microwave-safe bowl, heat the milk for 30 to 40 seconds, until it is lukewarm (98 to 105 degrees Fahrenheit). Add the granulated sugar and yeast and stir with a whisk until they're dissolved. Cover with a clean dish towel and let the yeast proof for 10 minutes.

3. While the yeast is proofing, make the filling: Combine the butter, brown sugar, granulated sugar, cinnamon, and vanilla in a medium bowl. Set aside.

4. Finish the dough: After the yeast has proofed, whisk in the melted butter, egg, and vanilla until fully combined. Add the salt. Then mix in the flour, 1 cup at a time. Knead the dough briefly in the bowl, until it forms a ball. Cover the bowl with a clean dish towel or plastic wrap and let rest for 10 minutes.

Scan for more tips!

40   JULIE'S EATS & TREATS COOKBOOK

5. Lightly flour a work surface and a rolling pin. Roll the dough out into an approximate 14-x-18-inch rectangle that is ¼ inch thick. Spread the filling over the entire surface of the dough. Beginning at the short side, roll the dough up. Use a serrated knife to cut the dough into 12 rolls (see Julie's Notes).

6. Place the cinnamon rolls in the baking dish, cut side down. Cover with a clean dish towel and let rise for about 50 minutes.

7. Preheat the oven to 350 degrees Fahrenheit.

8. Drizzle heavy cream over the rolls. Bake for 24 to 26 minutes, until the tops are lightly golden brown.

9. For the frosting, combine the butter, cream cheese, powdered sugar, vanilla, and a pinch of salt in a medium bowl. Mix with a hand mixer until it's combined and smooth. Frost the cinnamon rolls and serve warm.

JULIE'S Notes

The butter for the filling can be slightly warmer than room temperature. The softer the butter, the easier it will be to combine the filling. You don't want it melted, but it can be very soft. To do this, I heat the stick of butter in the microwave for 20 to 25 seconds, stopping every 5 seconds to flip the stick, end to end.

To cut the dough into 12 rolls of similar thickness, I use a serrated knife and lightly press it into the dough to create a guide for cutting. First I make a mark in the very middle, to divide the dough in half. Then I make a mark dividing each half into half, and then each half into three equal parts. Each roll will be about 1 inch thick.

Banana Bread, page 51

Muffins and Breads

Banana Chocolate Chip Muffins // 44

Blueberry Muffins // 47

Cruffins // 48

Banana Bread // 51

Pumpkin Bread // 52

Cheesy Garlic Bread Loaf // 55

Beer Bread // 56

Cheddar Biscuits // 59

Texas Roadhouse Rolls // 60

12 MUFFINS

PREP TIME: 15 MINS
COOK TIME: 25 MINS
TOTAL TIME: 40 MINS

BANANA CHOCOLATE CHIP *Muffins*

Your favorite homemade banana muffins are loaded here with chocolate chips for the perfect sweet touch.

INGREDIENTS

Nonstick cooking spray, optional
3 large bananas, mashed
½ cup white granulated sugar
1 egg, lightly beaten
⅓ cup salted butter, melted

1½ cups all-purpose flour
1 teaspoon baking soda
1 teaspoon baking powder
½ cup chocolate chips

INSTRUCTIONS

1. Preheat the oven to 425 degrees Fahrenheit. Line a 12-cup muffin pan with paper baking cups or spray them lightly with nonstick cooking spray.

2. In a large bowl, combine the bananas, sugar, and egg. Add the melted butter and stir until combined.

3. In a separate bowl, combine the flour, baking soda, and baking powder. Add the dry ingredients to the wet ingredients and stir until they're just combined. Add the chocolate chips and stir them in.

4. Using a ¼-cup measuring cup, pour the batter into the prepared muffin cups. Bake at 425 degrees Fahrenheit for 5 minutes. Then reduce the temperature to 350 degrees Fahrenheit and bake for 15 to 19 minutes, until a toothpick inserted in the center of a muffin comes out clean.

Scan for more tips!

14 TO 16 MUFFINS

BLUEBERRY *Muffins*

These muffins are golden brown on the top, with a sprinkle of sugar. Plus they're loaded with juicy, ripe blueberries.

PREP TIME: 15 MINS
COOK TIME: 23 MINS
TOTAL TIME: 38 MINS

INGREDIENTS

- 2½ cups all-purpose flour, plus 1 Tablespoon for the blueberries
- 1 Tablespoon baking powder
- ½ teaspoon baking soda
- ½ teaspoon salt
- ½ cup unsalted butter, melted
- 1 cup white granulated sugar, plus 1 Tablespoon for topping
- 2 eggs
- 1½ cups sour cream
- 3 Tablespoons milk
- 1 teaspoon vanilla extract
- 1¼ cups fresh blueberries

INSTRUCTIONS

1. Preheat the oven to 425 degrees Fahrenheit. Line the cups of two 12-cup standard muffin pans with paper liners (see Julie's Notes).

2. In a large bowl, whisk together the flour, baking powder, baking soda, and salt. In another large bowl, whisk together the melted butter, sugar, eggs, sour cream, milk, and vanilla. In a small bowl, toss the blueberries with the 1 Tablespoon flour until coated.

3. Add the flour mixture to the butter mixture and mix until just incorporated (do not overmix). The mixture will be thick. Fold the blueberries into the batter.

4. Fill the muffin liners with the batter, filling each one until almost full. You may have some batter left over. Sprinkle the remaining 1 Tablespoon granulated sugar evenly over all the muffins.

5. Bake the muffins at 425 degrees Fahrenheit for 5 minutes. Then reduce the heat to 350 degrees Fahrenheit and continue baking for 15 to 18 minutes, until the tops are golden brown and a toothpick inserted in the middle of a muffin comes out clean.

6. Let the muffins cool in the pan for 3 to 4 minutes before removing.

JULIE'S *Notes*

I recommend filling any empty muffin cups with a liner and a few tablespoons of water to promote even baking and help keep the pan from warping. Or if you have a 16-cup standard muffin pan, you can use it to bake all the muffins in one pan.

To store leftover muffins, let them cool completely, then place in an airtight container. They will keep for 2 days at room temperature, in the refrigerator for 3 to 4 days, or in the freezer for up to 2 months.

Scan for more tips!

MUFFINS AND BREADS

12 CRUFFINS

PREP TIME: 20 MINS

COOK TIME: 23 MINS

TOTAL TIME: 43 MINS

CRUFFINS

*A cruffin (**cr**escent + m**uffin**) is a crescent roll that is buttered, coated with cinnamon sugar, rolled, and cut, for a fun twist on a muffin. These light, flaky treats melt in your mouth.*

INGREDIENTS

Nonstick cooking spray
1 cup white granulated sugar
1 Tablespoon ground cinnamon
All-purpose flour, for rolling

3 (8-ounce) tubes refrigerated crescent roll dough
6 Tablespoons salted butter, softened

INSTRUCTIONS

1. Preheat the oven to 350 degrees Fahrenheit. Lightly spray a 12-cup muffin pan with nonstick cooking spray.

2. Whisk together the sugar and cinnamon in a small bowl.

3. Sprinkle a little flour on a work surface and, one at a time, roll out each tube of dough to a 12-x-16-inch rectangle.

4. Spread 2 Tablespoons of the softened butter evenly over each sheet of dough. Sprinkle ¼ cup of the cinnamon sugar evenly over the top of each buttered dough sheet. Gently press the cinnamon sugar into the dough. Set aside the remaining cinnamon sugar for later.

5. Starting on a long end of one dough sheet, tightly roll it up into a log. Cut the log in half, creating two shorter logs. Cut each of those shorter logs in half lengthwise, giving you four long sections of dough. Repeat with the remaining two sheets of dough. This will give you 12 long pieces of dough.

6. Working with one piece of dough at a time, with the cut sides facing out, roll it tightly into a round cinnamon roll shape. Place each cruffin in the prepared muffin pan, tucking the end piece of dough into the muffin cup.

7. Bake for 20 to 23 minutes, until the cruffins are golden brown on top and cooked through.

8. Remove from the oven and immediately roll each cruffin in the remaining cinnamon sugar mixture, covering all sides. Serve immediately.

BANANA *Bread*

This simple, easy-to-make banana bread is tender and moist. It was my mom's recipe, and I have so many great childhood memories of enjoying a warm slice with butter slathered on top.

SERVES 8

PREP TIME: 15 MINS
COOK TIME: 1 HR
TOTAL TIME: 1 HR 15 MINS

INGREDIENTS

- Nonstick cooking spray
- ¾ cup packed brown sugar
- 1 cup salted butter, softened
- 2 eggs
- 4 bananas, mashed
- 2 cups all-purpose flour
- 1 teaspoon baking soda
- ¼ teaspoon salt

INSTRUCTIONS

1. Preheat the oven to 350 degrees Fahrenheit. Spray a 9-x-5-inch loaf pan with nonstick cooking spray.

2. Combine the brown sugar and butter in a large bowl and beat with an electric beater until light and fluffy. Add the eggs and bananas and mix until combined. Add the flour, baking soda, and salt, and mix until just combined.

3. Pour the batter into the loaf pan. Bake for 1 hour, or until a toothpick inserted in the middle comes out clean.

Scan for more tips!

MUFFINS AND BREADS   51

SERVES 16

PREP TIME: 15 MINS
COOK TIME: 65 MINS
TOTAL TIME: 1 HR 20 MINS

PUMPKIN *Bread*

This recipe was my grandma's—I stole it out of my mom's recipe cards. It's tender, moist, and delicious, and loaded with warm spices.

INGREDIENTS

- Nonstick cooking spray
- 3⅓ cups all-purpose flour
- 3 cups white granulated sugar
- 2 teaspoons baking soda
- 1½ teaspoons salt
- 1 teaspoon ground cinnamon
- 1 teaspoon ground nutmeg
- 1 (15-ounce) can plain pumpkin purée
- 1 cup vegetable oil
- 4 eggs
- ⅔ cup water

INSTRUCTIONS

1. Preheat the oven to 350 degrees Fahrenheit. Spray two 9-x-5-inch loaf pans with nonstick cooking spray.
2. In a medium bowl, combine the flour, sugar, baking soda, salt, cinnamon, and nutmeg. In a large bowl, combine the pumpkin, oil, eggs, and water. Mix the dry ingredients into the wet ingredients and stir until combined. Spoon the batter into the loaf pans.
3. Bake for 60 to 65 minutes, until a toothpick inserted near the center comes out clean.
4. Cool in the pans for 10 minutes, then remove the loaves from the pans and let them cool on a wire rack.

JULIE'S *Notes*

This recipe makes two loaves, making it great to share with a friend, or freeze one for later. To freeze, wrap the loaf in heavy-duty aluminum foil or plastic wrap. Then place it in a resealable freezer bag, making sure to squeeze all the air out before sealing, and freeze for up to 3 months.

Scan for more tips!

CHEESY GARLIC BREAD *Loaf*

SERVES 8

PREP TIME: 10 MINS

COOK TIME: 15 MINS

TOTAL TIME: 25 MINS

My mom made this when we were growing up, and I still remember getting excited when I knew it was on the menu. She had a dump-and-guess recipe, but I wanted to share her cheesy, garlicky bread with you, so we went to work measuring and perfecting it.

INGREDIENTS

2 cups shredded mozzarella cheese

1 cup shredded cheddar cheese

½ cup salted butter, melted

1 Tablespoon dried parsley

2 teaspoons garlic powder

½ teaspoon paprika

1 loaf French bread

INSTRUCTIONS

1. Preheat the oven to 350 degrees Fahrenheit. Line a large baking sheet with aluminum foil.

2. In a large bowl, mix together both cheeses, the butter, parsley, garlic powder, and paprika.

3. Cut the French bread loaf in half lengthwise and place on the baking sheet. Spread the cheese mixture evenly on both cut sides of the bread.

4. Bake for 15 minutes, or until the cheese is melted and golden brown.

JULIE'S *Notes*

For the most "meltability," grab a block of cheese and grate it yourself!

SERVES 8

PREP TIME: 10 MINS

COOK TIME: 1 HR

TOTAL TIME: 1 HR 10 MINS

BEER *Bread*

Ditch the box mix and make beer bread from scratch with this easy and delicious recipe. The quick bread has only six ingredients and can be whipped together in one bowl with just a spoon.

INGREDIENTS

Nonstick cooking spray
3 cups all-purpose flour
⅓ cup white granulated sugar
1 Tablespoon baking powder
½ teaspoon salt
1 (12-ounce) can beer
3 Tablespoons salted butter, melted

INSTRUCTIONS

1. Preheat the oven to 350 degrees Fahrenheit. Spray a 9-x-5-inch loaf pan with nonstick cooking spray.

2. In a large bowl, combine the flour, sugar, baking powder, salt, and beer. The batter will be sticky. Do not overmix.

3. Spoon the batter into the prepared pan and pour the melted butter over the top. Bake for 50 to 60 minutes, or until golden brown on top.

JULIE'S *Notes*

You can use ginger ale in this recipe instead of beer, but it will lack the deep flavor the beer provides.

MIX-IN IDEAS:

GARLIC: Mince a few cloves of garlic and mix them into the batter.

CHEESE: Add a cup of shredded cheese to the batter. Any type of cheese, like cheddar or pepper jack, is fine.

HERBS: Add minced fresh herbs, like rosemary or thyme. Dried herbs will also work.

SPICE: Add sliced jalapeño peppers or green chilies for some heat—and cheddar cheese, too, for a fun twist.

Scan for more tips!

12 BISCUITS

CHEDDAR *Biscuits*

These easy drop biscuits are light and fluffy. Flavored with garlic and cheddar cheese, they make the perfect side dish for any dinner.

PREP TIME: 10 MINS
COOK TIME: 15 MINS
TOTAL TIME: 25 MINS

INGREDIENTS

- Nonstick cooking spray
- 2 cups all-purpose baking mix (see Julie's Notes)
- 1 cup shredded cheddar cheese
- 4 cloves garlic, minced, divided
- ⅔ cup milk, cold
- 2 Tablespoons salted butter
- 1 Tablespoon chopped fresh parsley

INSTRUCTIONS

1. Preheat the oven to 400 degrees Fahrenheit. Spray a large baking sheet with nonstick cooking spray.

2. In a large bowl, combine the baking mix, cheddar cheese, and half the minced garlic. Stir in the milk and mix. Drop the batter by heaping spoonfuls onto the baking sheet. It should make about 12 biscuits. Bake for 10 minutes.

3. Meanwhile, melt the butter in a small skillet and add the remaining minced garlic. Sauté over low heat for about 1 minute. Remove from the heat and stir in the parsley.

4. After 10 minutes of baking, brush the biscuits with the garlic butter and bake for 5 minutes more, or until they're golden brown on the bottom.

JULIE'S *Notes*

For the baking mix, we use Bisquick.

Scan for more tips!

MUFFINS AND BREADS

24 ROLLS

PREP TIME: 20 MINS

COOK TIME: 2 HRS

TOTAL TIME: 2 HRS 20 MINS

TEXAS ROADHOUSE Rolls

Copycat Texas Roadhouse Rolls are light, tender, and fluffy. Brush them with butter after baking to melt in your mouth.

INGREDIENTS

- 1¼ cups warm milk (105 to 110 degrees Fahrenheit)
- ⅓ cup white granulated sugar
- 1 (¼-ounce) package (2¼ teaspoons) active dry yeast
- ¼ cup unsalted butter, room temperature; plus 3 Tablespoons unsalted butter, melted
- 1 egg, room temperature
- 1 teaspoon salt
- 3½ to 4 cups all-purpose flour, plus more for kneading
- Nonstick cooking spray, optional

INSTRUCTIONS

1. Combine the milk and sugar in a small bowl. Sprinkle the yeast over and let sit until it's foamy, about 5 minutes.

2. Transfer the yeast mixture to a large bowl. Add the butter, egg, salt, and 2 cups of the flour. Using a handheld or standing mixer, beat the mixture on medium speed until the batter is smooth. Gradually add 1½ cups more flour until a soft ball of dough forms. Then increase the speed to medium-high and beat for 2 to 3 minutes longer. The dough should be tacky but not sticky. If it's too sticky, add more flour, 1 Tablespoon at a time.

3. Lightly grease a large bowl. Gather the dough into a ball and place it in the bowl, turning once to coat. Cover the bowl with a clean dish towel and set in a warm place to rise until the dough has doubled in size, 45 to 60 minutes.

4. Punch the dough down gently. Lightly flour a work surface and turn the dough out of the bowl. Knead briefly, if necessary. (Stretch a section of dough between your fingers. If the dough tears, it needs to be kneaded more. If it stretches without tearing—making a windowpane of sorts—your dough is ready.)

5. Let the dough sit a few minutes while you prepare two rimmed 10-x-15-inch baking sheets by lining them with a silicone baking mat or spraying with nonstick cooking spray.

JULIE'S Notes

Store leftover rolls in an airtight container at room temperature up to 3 days. To freeze, place baked rolls on baking sheet and freeze, then transfer to a freezer bag or airtight container. They will last in the freezer for up to 3 months.

Scan for more tips!

60   JULIE'S EATS & TREATS COOKBOOK

6. Roll the dough out into a 12-x-8-inch rectangle, ½ inch thick. Using a sharp knife, cut the dough into 2-inch squares to make 24 rolls. Transfer the rolls to the prepared baking sheets. Cover with a dish towel and let the rolls rise in a warm place until they are almost doubled in size, 45 to 60 minutes.

7. About 20 minutes before baking, preheat the oven to 350 degrees Fahrenheit.

8. Bake the rolls for 12 to 15 minutes, until golden brown. Remove from the oven, brush with the melted butter, and serve.

Oven Roasted Vegetables, page 91

Salads and Sides

Tossed Salad with Italian Dressing // 64

Pea Salad // 67

Potato Salad // 68

Macaroni Salad // 71

Dorito Taco Salad // 72

Oreo Fluff // 75

Strawberry Pretzel Salad // 76

Fried Rice // 79

Spanish Rice // 80

Cheesy Garlic-Butter Pasta // 83

Roasted Sweet Potatoes // 84

Cheesy Bacon Ranch Potatoes // 87

Funeral Potatoes // 88

Oven-Roasted Vegetables // 91

Bacon-Wrapped Green Beans // 92

SERVES 6

PREP TIME: 15 MINS

TOTAL TIME: 15 MINS

TOSSED SALAD *with* ITALIAN DRESSING

Here's a simple tossed salad with a delicious homemade dressing (or use store-bought Italian dressing if you like). The best thing about it is that it goes with almost any main dish.

INGREDIENTS

8 cups roughly chopped iceberg lettuce

2 cups roughly chopped radicchio

2 cups cherry tomatoes, halved

¼ red onion, thinly sliced

½ cup black olives, pitted and halved

4 pepperoncini peppers, sliced

2 cups croutons

½ cup (or to taste) Italian dressing, homemade (below) or store-bought

½ cup grated parmesan cheese, or to taste

INSTRUCTIONS

1. Combine lettuce and radicchio in a large bowl. Add the tomatoes, red onion, olives, peppers, and croutons and toss gently.

2. Pour on the amount of dressing you like and toss to combine. Top with parmesan cheese and serve immediately.

GENEROUS 1/2 CUP

HOMEMADE ITALIAN DRESSING

INGREDIENTS

½ cup olive oil

2 Tablespoons red wine vinegar

1 teaspoon honey

1 teaspoon dried Italian seasoning

½ teaspoon salt

½ teaspoon garlic powder

¼ teaspoon ground black pepper

INSTRUCTIONS

Mix all the ingredients in a bottle and shake until thoroughly combined.

JULIE'S *Notes*

Store in an airtight container in the refrigerator for up to three weeks.

PEA Salad

Old-fashioned classic pea salad is a favorite that is perfect for holidays, potlucks, picnics, BBQs, and so much more. This one has cubed cheddar, bacon, and red onion, all tossed with a creamy dressing.

SERVES 8

PREP TIME: 15 MINS
CHILL TIME: 1 HR
TOTAL TIME: 1 HR 15 MINS

INGREDIENTS

DRESSING
- ½ cup sour cream
- ¼ cup mayonnaise
- 1 Tablespoon white granulated sugar
- 2 teaspoons white vinegar
- ½ teaspoon salt
- ¼ teaspoon ground black pepper

SALAD
- 8 slices bacon, cooked until crispy, drained, and chopped, plus more for garnish
- 6 ounces cheddar cheese, cut into small cubes, plus more for garnish
- 4 cups (about 24 ounces) frozen green peas, thawed
- ½ small red onion, finely diced

INSTRUCTIONS

1. To make the dressing, in a large serving bowl, whisk together all the dressing ingredients until thoroughly combined.

2. Add the bacon, cheese, peas, and onion to the dressing and gently toss to coat. Cover and refrigerate for at least 1 hour before serving.

3. Garnish with additional cheese and crumbled bacon just before serving.

Scan for more tips!

SALADS AND SIDES

SERVES 5

PREP TIME: 20 MINS

COOK TIME: 7 MINS

CHILL TIME: 1 HR

TOTAL TIME: 1 HR 27 MINS

POTATO *Salad*

My husband's grandma made the best potato salad ever. Of course, she never measured things—she just dumped and tasted. We developed this recipe and got it as close to hers as possible. It's a basic recipe, so feel free to mix in more ingredients (see Julie's Notes).

INGREDIENTS

5 pounds red potatoes, peeled and diced

2 cups mayonnaise or Miracle Whip

2 Tablespoons white vinegar

2 Tablespoons yellow mustard

1 teaspoon salt

1 teaspoon garlic powder

1 teaspoon onion powder

¼ teaspoon ground black pepper

6 hard-boiled eggs, peeled, divided

½ teaspoon paprika

Optional garnish: Sliced green onions

INSTRUCTIONS

1. Place the potatoes in a large pot and cover with water. Bring to a rapid boil over high heat, then turn the heat down to medium and boil for 5 to 7 minutes, until the potatoes are tender. Drain and let the potatoes cool.

2. In a medium bowl, combine the mayonnaise, vinegar, mustard, salt, garlic powder, onion powder, and pepper. Mix until combined. Pour the mixture over the cooled potatoes.

3. Dice three of the hard-boiled eggs and add to the potatoes. Gently mix until combined.

4. Slice the remaining three hard-boiled eggs and arrange the slices on top of the salad. Sprinkle with the paprika for garnish.

5. Cover and refrigerate until the salad is thoroughly cooled, about 1 hour or overnight.

JULIE'S *Notes*

Great add-ins to this basic recipe include diced red onion, pickle relish, diced celery, and chopped fresh dill.

MACARONI *Salad*

This classic creamy salad is a hit with both kids and adults at potlucks, parties, and BBQs. It has tons of flavor from peas, ham, cheese, and seasonings.

SERVES 4

PREP TIME: 10 MINS
COOK TIME: 12 MINS
CHILL TIME: 1 HR
TOTAL TIME: 1 HR 22 MINS

INGREDIENTS

- 1 pound uncooked elbow macaroni
- 2 cups mayonnaise
- ¾ teaspoon yellow mustard
- 1 teaspoon onion salt
- ½ teaspoon celery salt
- ¼ teaspoon seasoning salt
- 1 pound frozen peas, rinsed under warm water
- 8 ounces shredded cheddar cheese
- 1 cup diced ham

INSTRUCTIONS

1. Cook the macaroni in a large pot of boiling water according to the package directions. Drain, rinse with cold water, and set aside.

2. In a large bowl, mix together the mayonnaise, mustard, onion salt, celery salt, and seasoning salt. Add the cooked pasta, peas, cheddar cheese, and ham. Mix well.

3. Cover and chill in the fridge for least 1 hour before serving.

JULIE'S *Notes*

If the pasta salad soaks up the dressing and is dry when you are ready to serve it, mix in a little extra mayonnaise.

Scan for more tips!

SALADS AND SIDES

SERVES 12

PREP TIME: 15 MINS

COOK TIME: 10 MINS

TOTAL TIME: 25 MINS

DORITO TACO *Salad*

I still ask my mom to make this for me. It's a delicious mixture of taco meat, cheese, lettuce, tomatoes, onions, and nacho cheese Doritos. It's the perfect potluck salad, and it's also great for an easy summer meal.

INGREDIENTS

1½ pounds ground beef

1 (1-ounce) package taco seasoning

⅔ cup water

1 head iceberg lettuce, chopped

2 tomatoes, chopped

1 yellow onion, chopped

2 cups shredded cheddar cheese

1 (16-ounce) bottle Catalina dressing

1 (15.5-ounce) bag nacho cheese Doritos, crushed

INSTRUCTIONS

1. In a large skillet, brown the ground beef over medium-high heat for 5 to 7 minutes, or until cooked through. Drain off the grease. Stir in the taco seasoning and water. Simmer until thickened, about 5 minutes. Set aside to cool.

2. In a large bowl, mix the cooled ground beef with the lettuce, tomatoes, onion, and cheddar cheese. Refrigerate until you're ready to serve, up to 24 hours.

3. Right before serving, pour on the dressing, toss, and mix in the crushed Doritos.

JULIE'S *Notes*

If you are not going to enjoy the salad all at one time, simply take out the amount you'd like, top with dressing and chips, and store the rest of the salad in an airtight container in the fridge for 3–4 days.

OREO *Fluff*

This light, fluffy cookie "salad," made with crushed Oreos, Cool Whip, and instant pudding mix, takes only 15 minutes to whip up. It's always a hit wherever you take it. (And yes, in the Midwest, this is officially a salad!)

SERVES 12

PREP TIME: 15 MINS
CHILL TIME: 1 HR
TOTAL TIME: 1 HR 15 MINS

INGREDIENTS

- 2 cups buttermilk
- 2 (4.2-ounce) boxes Jell-O Cookies 'n Creme instant pudding mix
- 1 (16-ounce) container Cool Whip, thawed
- 1 (14.3-ounce) package Oreos, chopped, divided

INSTRUCTIONS

1. In a large bowl, whip together the buttermilk, pudding mix, and Cool Whip.
2. Set aside 1 cup of the chopped Oreos for garnish and add the rest to the bowl. Stir until combined.
3. Cover and refrigerate until you're ready to serve—at least 1 hour or overnight.
4. Sprinkle with the reserved Oreos right before serving.

JULIE'S *Notes*

I hope you enjoy this easy recipe as much as my dear friend Abbie. It's the go-to easy side for both of us. This one's for you!

Scan for more tips!

SALADS AND SIDES

SERVES 12

PREP TIME: 20 MINS
COOK TIME: 10 MINS
CHILL TIME: 4 HRS 30 MINS
TOTAL TIME: 5 HRS

STRAWBERRY PRETZEL *Salad*

A crunchy pretzel crust topped with a layer of sweet cream cheese and Cool Whip, with fresh strawberries and Jell-O on top: What could be better? Serve this delicious concoction as a salad or a dessert.

INGREDIENTS

JELL-O LAYER
- 1 (6-ounce) box Jell-O strawberry gelatin mix
- 2 cups boiling water
- 1 pound fresh strawberries, thinly sliced

PRETZEL CRUST
- 2½ cups crushed pretzels
- ¼ cup white granulated sugar
- ½ cup salted butter, melted

CREAM CHEESE LAYER
- 1 (8-ounce) package cream cheese, softened
- ¾ cup white granulated sugar
- 1 (8-ounce) container Cool Whip, thawed

INSTRUCTIONS

1. In a small bowl, combine the Jell-O mix with the boiling water. Whisk until the gelatin is dissolved. Let cool until it is at room temperature, about an hour.
2. Preheat the oven to 350 degrees Fahrenheit.
3. Prepare the pretzel crust: Mix together the crushed pretzels, sugar, and melted butter in a large bowl until combined. Press into the bottom of a 9-x-13-inch baking pan. Bake the crust for 10 minutes. Let cool.
4. Prepare the cream cheese layer: In a large bowl, beat the cream cheese with the sugar until smooth. Fold in the Cool Whip. Spread over the cooled pretzel crust. Make sure to get it all the way to the edge to prevent the strawberry layer from running into the other layers. Refrigerate for 30 minutes.
5. Place the sliced strawberries on top of the cream cheese layer. *Slowly* pour the Jell-O mixture over the strawberries. Refrigerate until set, 4 to 6 hours or until firm. To serve, remove from the refrigerator and cut into slices.
6. Store any leftovers in the refrigerator.

JULIE'S *Notes*

You can substitute 10 ounces thawed frozen strawberries for the fresh strawberries.

Scan for more tips!

76 JULIE'S EATS & TREATS COOKBOOK

Fried RICE

This delicious homemade fried rice is the perfect quick side when you have leftover rice on hand. And nothing goes better with your favorite Chinese-style recipes than fresh, steaming fried rice.

PREP TIME: 5 MINS

COOK TIME: 10 MINS

TOTAL TIME: 15 MINS

SERVES 4

INGREDIENTS

- 3 Tablespoons sesame oil
- 1 cup frozen peas and carrots, thawed
- 1 small yellow onion, chopped
- 2 teaspoons minced garlic
- 2 eggs, lightly beaten
- 3 cups cooked white rice (see Julie's Notes)
- ¼ cup soy sauce
- Optional garnish: Sliced green onions

INSTRUCTIONS

1. Heat the oil in a large skillet or wok over medium-high heat. Add the peas and carrots, onion, and garlic and stir-fry until the vegetables are tender, about 5 minutes.

2. Reduce the heat to medium-low and push the vegetables off to one side. Pour the eggs on the other side of the skillet and stir-fry until they're scrambled.

3. Add the rice and soy sauce and blend everything together well. Stir-fry until thoroughly heated, 4 to 5 minutes longer.

JULIE'S Notes

Day-old or leftover rice works best.

SALADS AND SIDES

SERVES 4

PREP TIME: 5 MINS
COOK TIME: 35 MINS
TOTAL TIME: 40 MINS

Spanish RICE

This quick and easy rice is a Midwestern twist on the traditional dish. The combination of white rice, onion, and salsa creates the perfect side for any of your Mexican-style dishes.

INGREDIENTS

2 Tablespoons vegetable oil
½ cup chopped yellow onion
1½ cups uncooked white rice

2 cups chicken broth
1 cup salsa

INSTRUCTIONS

1. Heat the oil in a large skillet over medium heat. Stir in the onion and cook until tender, about 5 minutes. Add the rice and cook, stirring often, until beginning to brown, 4 to 5 minutes.

2. Stir in the chicken broth and salsa. Reduce the heat, cover, and simmer for 20 to 25 minutes, until the liquid has been absorbed and the rice is cooked through.

Scan for more tips!

80   JULIE'S EATS & TREATS COOKBOOK

Cheesy GARLIC-BUTTER PASTA

PREP TIME: 5 MINS
COOK TIME: 13 MINS
TOTAL TIME: 18 MINS

SERVES 4

You can never beat the combo of garlic, cheese, and pasta. These noodles come together in less than 20 minutes and make a perfect partner to any main dish.

INGREDIENTS

- 2¼ cups uncooked shell pasta
- ⅔ cup shredded mozzarella cheese
- 2 Tablespoons salted butter, melted
- 2 Tablespoons grated parmesan cheese
- 2 teaspoons minced fresh parsley
- ¼ teaspoon salt
- ¼ teaspoon garlic powder
- ⅛ teaspoon ground black pepper

INSTRUCTIONS

1. Cook the pasta in a large pot of boiling salted water according to the package directions; drain. Return the pasta to the pot.
2. Add all the remaining ingredients and mix until the cheese is melted.

Scan for more tips!

SALADS AND SIDES

SERVES 4

PREP TIME: 15 MINS
COOK TIME: 30 MINS
TOTAL TIME: 45 MINS

Roasted SWEET POTATOES

Here's a quick and easy side dish that's perfect for busy nights. Diced sweet potatoes are seasoned and roasted for a caramelized crust and a soft center.

INGREDIENTS

- 3 sweet potatoes, peeled and cut into ½-inch dice
- 2 Tablespoons olive oil
- 2 teaspoons smoked paprika
- 1 teaspoon garlic salt
- ½ teaspoon ground black pepper

INSTRUCTIONS

1. Preheat the oven to 425 degrees Fahrenheit.
2. Spread the sweet potatoes on a 13-x-18-inch baking sheet. Pour the olive oil over and toss to coat. Sprinkle with the paprika, garlic salt, and pepper and toss until the potatoes are seasoned. Spread the potatoes out so they are not overlapping.
3. Roast for 30 minutes, flipping the potatoes every 10 minutes for even browning, until the potatoes are fork tender and the edges are caramelized.

JULIE'S Notes

Make sure to spread the potatoes out on the baking sheet. If they overlap, you will steam them and not roast them.

Scan for more tips!

Cheesy BACON RANCH POTATOES

SERVES 6

PREP TIME: 15 MINS
COOK TIME: 1 HR 5 MINS
TOTAL TIME: 1 HR 20 MINS

Ranch, bacon, and cheddar—that's a combo that Minnesotans just can't resist. So go ahead and layer potatoes with ranch dressing, cheddar cheese, and bacon bits for a quick and easy side dish.

INGREDIENTS

- Nonstick cooking spray
- 3 pounds Yukon gold potatoes, washed and cubed (see Julie's Notes)
- ¼ cup salted butter, cubed
- ¼ cup Hormel real bacon bits
- ¼ cup ranch dressing
- ½ cup shredded cheddar cheese

INSTRUCTIONS

1. Preheat the oven to 400 degrees Fahrenheit. Lightly spray an 8-x-8-inch glass baking dish with nonstick cooking spray.
2. Put the potatoes in the baking dish and scatter the butter cubes on top. Sprinkle the bacon bits on top.
3. Cover with aluminum foil and bake for 1 hour, or until the potatoes are fork tender.
4. Top with the ranch dressing and cheese and stir. Return to the oven and bake, uncovered, until the cheese is melted, about 5 minutes.

JULIE'S *Notes*

I don't peel the potatoes, but you can if you want.

Scan for more tips!

SALADS AND SIDES 87

SERVES 8

PREP TIME: 15 MINS

COOK TIME: 1 HR

TOTAL TIME: 1 HR 15 MINS

Funeral **POTATOES**

This quick and easy hash brown casserole, loaded with cheese, is great for an easy side dish. It got its name because it is often served at after-funeral luncheons.

INGREDIENTS

POTATOES
Nonstick cooking spray

1 (10¾-ounce) can condensed cream of chicken soup

2 cups sour cream

2 cups shredded sharp cheddar cheese

½ cup milk

½ cup salted butter, melted

1 (30-ounce) package frozen shredded hash browns, thawed

TOPPING
1 cup cornflakes

¼ cup grated parmesan cheese

2 Tablespoons salted butter, melted

Optional garnish: Chopped parsley

INSTRUCTIONS

1. Preheat the oven to 350 degrees Fahrenheit. Spray a 13-x-9-inch baking dish with nonstick cooking spray.

2. In a large bowl, combine the soup, sour cream, cheddar cheese, milk, and butter. Stir in the hash browns and transfer to the baking dish.

3. In a medium bowl, combine all the topping ingredients. Sprinkle over the top of the hash brown mixture.

4. Bake, uncovered, for 50 to 60 minutes, until the top is golden brown and the edges are bubbling.

Oven-Roasted VEGETABLES

SERVES 5

PREP TIME: 15 MINS
COOK TIME: 40 MINS
TOTAL TIME: 55 MINS

These delicious and easy roasted vegetables are a great side dish. I love making a big batch on the weekend and having them for lunch throughout the week. Onions, sweet potatoes, red onions, zucchini, and carrots are drizzled in balsamic vinegar, seasoned, and roasted to perfection in the oven.

INGREDIENTS

- 2 sweet potatoes, peeled and cubed
- 1 cup cubed Yukon gold potatoes
- 1 red onion, quartered
- 1 zucchini, cut into 1-inch cubes
- 3 carrots, peeled and cut into 1½-inch chunks
- ½ pound Brussels sprouts, outer leaves removed, halved
- 6 cloves garlic, minced
- 1 teaspoon sea salt
- ½ teaspoon ground black pepper
- 2 Tablespoons olive oil
- 2 Tablespoons balsamic vinegar

INSTRUCTIONS

1. Preheat the oven to 400 degrees Fahrenheit.
2. Place all the prepared vegetables in one even layer on a 11-x-17-inch baking sheet or two smaller pans with rims. Make sure they are not overlapping. Sprinkle with the garlic, salt, and pepper, then drizzle on the olive oil and balsamic vinegar. Toss to combine until all the vegetables are coated.
3. Roast on the middle rack, flipping the vegetables halfway through the baking time, until the vegetables are turning brown and crispy at their edges and tender inside, 35 to 40 minutes.

Scan for more tips!

SERVES 5

PREP TIME: 20 MINS
COOK TIME: 30 MINS
TOTAL TIME: 50 MINS

Bacon-Wrapped GREEN BEANS

Bacony green beans are the perfect side dish. Tender, crisp green beans are brushed with a simple glaze, wrapped in bacon, and then baked. They can even be prepped ahead of time for easy entertaining (see Julie's Notes).

INGREDIENTS

- 10 slices bacon (not thick-cut)
- 1 pound green beans, ends trimmed
- ¼ cup salted butter, melted
- 2 Tablespoons brown sugar
- 1 teaspoon garlic salt
- ½ teaspoon ground black pepper
- Nonstick cooking spray
- 1 Tablespoon chopped fresh parsley, optional

INSTRUCTIONS

1. Preheat the oven to 400 degrees Fahrenheit. Line a large baking sheet with aluminum foil.

2. Place the bacon on the baking sheet and bake for about 10 minutes. The bacon will not be fully cooked. Leave the oven on.

3. Bring a large pot of water to a boil. Add the green beans and cook for 2 to 3 minutes, until just tender. Drain the beans and place in a bowl of ice water to stop the cooking. Drain again, pat dry, and transfer to a large bowl.

4. In a small bowl, mix together the butter, brown sugar, garlic salt, and pepper. Pour the mixture over the green beans and toss to coat.

5. Line another large baking sheet with aluminum foil or spray it with nonstick cooking spray.

6. Gather up 8 to 10 green beans and place them crosswise on one end of a slice of bacon. Roll the green beans up in the bacon. Place the bundle, seam side down, on the baking sheet. Repeat with the rest of the green beans and bacon.

7. Bake for 15 to 20 minutes, until the bacon is crispy. Sprinkle with the parsley, if desired, and serve immediately.

JULIE'S Notes

French green beans or thinner green beans work best for this dish.

The bacon and green bean rolls can be prepped a day ahead. Place them on the baking sheet, cover with plastic wrap, and keep it in the refrigerator for up to 1 day.

Scan for more tips!

Creamy Chicken Noodle Soup, page 100

Soups and Stews

Broccoli Cheese Soup // 96

Chicken and Rice Soup // 99

Creamy Chicken Noodle Soup // 100

Chicken and Wild Rice Soup // 103

Hamburger Soup // 104

Sausage and Potato Soup // 107

Lasagna Soup // 108

Chili // 111

Slow Cooker White Chicken Chili // 112

Slow Cooker Enchilada Soup // 115

Slow Cooker Zuppa Toscana // 116

Slow Cooker Beef Stew // 119

SERVES 6

PREP TIME: 10 MINS
COOK TIME: 30 MINS
TOTAL TIME: 40 MINS

BROCCOLI CHEESE *Soup*

Make your favorite cheesy, rich, and creamy soup at home with fresh broccoli.

INGREDIENTS

½ cup unsalted butter
1 yellow onion, chopped
½ cup all-purpose flour
4 cups low-sodium chicken broth
4 cups half-and-half
1 teaspoon garlic powder
½ teaspoon paprika
½ teaspoon dry mustard
Salt and ground black pepper to taste
4 cups broccoli florets or chopped broccoli
2 cups diced carrots
3 cups shredded sharp cheddar cheese

INSTRUCTIONS

1. In a Dutch oven or soup pot, melt the butter over medium-high heat. Add the onion and sauté until soft and translucent, 2 to 3 minutes. Add the flour and continue to cook, whisking often, to create a roux, about a minute, or until it takes on a light tan color and is slightly thickened.

2. Continue whisking as you pour in about half of the broth. When it is incorporated, add the remaining broth, whisking all the while. Then slowly whisk in the half-and-half. Cook for another 2 to 3 minutes, whisking often to get out all the lumps. Add the garlic powder, paprika, dry mustard, salt, and pepper and whisk to combine.

3. Remove the pot from the heat and transfer the soup to a blender or food processor, or use an immersion blender directly in the pot, and blend until smooth. (This step is optional.)

4. Return the soup to the pot and add the broccoli florets and carrots. Reduce the heat to medium-low and simmer for 15 to 20 minutes, stirring occasionally, until the soup has thickened and the vegetables are fork tender.

5. Add the cheddar cheese a handful at a time, stirring to incorporate after each handful. Season with more salt and pepper as needed and serve immediately.

JULIE'S *Notes*

You can substitute vegetable broth for the chicken broth.

Serve with Cheddar Biscuits (page 59) or Beer Bread (page 56).

Scan for more tips!

CHICKEN AND RICE *Soup*

SERVES 4

This is a quick and easy soup with carrots, shredded chicken, rice, and seasonings. It's perfectly creamy, hearty, and like a big hug in a bowl for a cozy dinner.

PREP TIME: 15 MINS
COOK TIME: 30 MINS
TOTAL TIME: 45 MINS

INGREDIENTS

- 1 Tablespoon olive oil
- 1 yellow onion, minced
- 3 large carrots, peeled and diced
- 2 ribs celery, diced
- 1 teaspoon minced garlic
- 1 teaspoon dried parsley
- ½ teaspoon dried thyme
- 1 teaspoon salt
- ¼ teaspoon ground black pepper
- 6 cups low-sodium chicken broth
- 1 pound skinless boneless chicken breasts
- 1 cup uncooked white rice
- 1 cup evaporated milk

INSTRUCTIONS

1. In a large Dutch oven or soup pot, heat the oil over medium-high heat. Add the onion, carrots, and celery and cook and stir for 4 to 5 minutes, until the onion begins to turn golden brown. Add the garlic, parsley, and thyme and cook for 1 minute. Add the salt and pepper, broth, chicken breasts, and rice and stir to combine. Bring to a boil over medium-high heat.

2. Reduce the heat to a simmer, cover, and cook for 18 to 20 minutes, stirring occasionally. The rice and vegetables should be tender and the internal temperature of the chicken breasts should be 165 degrees Fahrenheit.

3. Remove the chicken from the pot and shred using two forks. Return the chicken to the pot and stir in the evaporated milk. Heat through before serving.

JULIE'S *Notes*

Serve with Cheddar Biscuits (page 59) or Beer Bread (page 56).

Scan for more tips!

SOUPS AND STEWS

SERVES 6

PREP TIME: 15 MINS
COOK TIME: 45 MINS
TOTAL TIME: 1 HR

CREAMY CHICKEN NOODLE *Soup*

This easy soup has a creamy base and lots of chicken, carrots, celery, and egg noodles. It's a delicious, creamy twist on classic chicken noodle soup that will warm you from the inside out!

INGREDIENTS

- 1 Tablespoon olive oil
- 4 carrots, peeled and chopped
- 3 ribs celery, diced
- ½ yellow onion, chopped
- 1 teaspoon minced garlic
- ½ cup all-purpose flour
- 8 cups low-sodium chicken broth
- 1 pound skinless boneless chicken breasts
- 3 cups uncooked wide egg noodles
- 1 (12-ounce) can evaporated milk
- 1 teaspoon salt
- ½ teaspoon ground black pepper
- ¼ teaspoon dried oregano

INSTRUCTIONS

1. Heat the oil over medium-high heat in a Dutch oven or a large stockpot. Add the carrots, celery, and onion and sauté until they're beginning to soften, about 7 minutes. Add the garlic and cook for an additional 1 minute.

2. Sprinkle the flour over the vegetables and cook for 1 minute, stirring continually. Slowly stir in the broth. Add the chicken, bring the liquid to a boil, and reduce the heat. Simmer, partially covered, for 20 minutes.

3. Stir in the noodles, evaporated milk, salt, pepper, and oregano. Stir to combine and cook the soup for 10 minutes, or until the noodles are al dente.

4. Remove the chicken, shred, and return it to the pot. Heat through before serving.

JULIE'S *Notes*

Serve with Cheddar Biscuits (page 59) or Beer Bread (page 56).

Scan for more tips!

100 JULIE'S EATS & TREATS COOKBOOK

CHICKEN AND WILD RICE *Soup*

This creamy soup, loaded with chicken, carrots, celery, mushrooms, and more delicious ingredients, is so easy to make because it's all prepared in one pot, making it perfect for an easy meal.

PREP TIME: 15 MINS
COOK TIME: 30 MINS
TOTAL TIME: 45 MINS

SERVES 6

INGREDIENTS

- ½ cup salted butter
- 1 medium yellow onion, chopped
- 1 carrot, peeled and finely chopped
- 1 rib celery, finely chopped
- ½ cup chopped mushrooms
- ½ cup all-purpose flour
- 3 cups low-sodium chicken broth
- 2 cups cooked wild rice
- 2 cups shredded cooked chicken
- ½ teaspoon garlic powder
- ½ teaspoon salt
- 2 cups half-and-half
- Chopped fresh parsley, for garnish

INSTRUCTIONS

1. In a large Dutch oven or soup pot, melt the butter over medium-high heat. Stir in the onion, carrot, celery, and mushrooms and sauté for 5 to 7 minutes, until tender.

2. Slowly add the flour, stirring constantly so it does not clump together. Gradually whisk in the broth. Cook, stirring constantly, until the mixture comes to a boil. Boil for 1 minute. Stir in the cooked wild rice, chicken, garlic powder, and salt. Simmer for 5 minutes.

3. Slowly blend in the half-and-half, then lower the heat to low and simmer for about 10 minutes. Garnish with the parsley and serve.

JULIE'S *Notes*

Serve with Cheddar Biscuits (page 59) or Beer Bread (page 56).

Scan for more tips!

SOUPS AND STEWS

SERVES 6

PREP TIME: 15 MINS
COOK TIME: 40 MINS
TOTAL TIME: 55 MINS

HAMBURGER *Soup*

This easy soup combines ground beef, vegetables, canned tomatoes, and potatoes. It's the perfect soup for those chilly nights when you are craving something wholesome and heartwarming.

INGREDIENTS

- 1½ teaspoons olive oil
- 1 medium yellow onion, diced
- 2 ribs celery, chopped
- 2 carrots, peeled and chopped
- 3 cloves garlic, minced
- 1 pound extra-lean ground beef
- 6 cups low-sodium beef broth
- 1 (14.5-ounce) can petite diced tomatoes
- 1 (8-ounce) can tomato sauce
- 2 teaspoons Worcestershire sauce
- 2 large russet potatoes, peeled and diced
- ½ cup frozen corn
- ½ cup frozen green beans
- 1 teaspoon salt
- ½ teaspoon ground black pepper
- ½ teaspoon dried Italian seasoning

INSTRUCTIONS

1. Heat the oil in a large Dutch oven or stock pot over medium heat Add the onion, celery, and carrots and sauté for 5 to 7 minutes, until softened.

2. Stir in the garlic and sauté for 1 minute. Add the ground beef and cook until the beef has browned, about 5 minutes. Drain off the grease.

3. Stir in the broth, canned tomatoes, tomato sauce, Worcestershire sauce, potatoes, corn, green beans, salt, pepper, and Italian seasoning. Increase the heat and bring the soup to a boil. Then reduce the heat so it simmers and cook for 20 to 25 minutes, until the potatoes are tender.

JULIE'S *Notes*

You can substitute ground turkey for the ground beef.

Serve with Cheddar Biscuits (page 59) or Beer Bread (page 56).

Scan for more tips!

104 JULIE'S EATS & TREATS COOKBOOK

SAUSAGE AND POTATO *Soup*

SERVES 4

This delicious, creamy soup has so much flavor from Italian sausage and seasonings. Serve a bowl with a piece of crusty bread for dunking.

PREP TIME: 20 MINS

COOK TIME: 30 MINS

TOTAL TIME: 50 MINS

INGREDIENTS

- 1 pound ground Italian sausage
- ¾ cup chopped yellow onion
- 3 carrots, peeled and diced
- 3 ribs celery, diced
- 1 Tablespoon minced garlic
- 1 teaspoon dried basil
- 1 teaspoon dried parsley
- ¾ teaspoon salt

- ½ teaspoon dried oregano
- ¼ teaspoon ground black pepper
- 1¼ pounds Yukon gold potatoes (about 6 medium potatoes), peeled and diced
- 5 cups chicken broth
- 1 cup heavy cream
- 3 Tablespoons cornstarch
- 1½ cups shredded sharp cheddar cheese

INSTRUCTIONS

1. In a large pot over medium-high heat, brown the sausage meat for 2 to 3 minutes. Add the onions, carrots, and celery and continue to cook and stir until the onion is just translucent, 2 to 3 minutes. Add the garlic, basil, parsley, salt, oregano, and pepper and stir to combine.

2. Add the potatoes and pour in the chicken broth. Bring the soup to a boil and cover with a lid. Reduce the heat and simmer, stirring occasionally, until the potatoes are tender, 10 to 12 minutes.

3. In a small bowl, combine the cream and cornstarch. Pour the mixture into the soup while stirring. Bring the soup back to a slow boil and continue to stir until the soup thickens, 2 to 3 minutes.

4. Turn off the heat and add the cheese, stirring until it's melted and combined.

JULIE'S *Notes*

Serve with Cheddar Biscuits (page 59) or Beer Bread (page 56).

SERVES 4

PREP TIME: 10 MINS
COOK TIME: 30 MINS
TOTAL TIME: 40 MINS

LASAGNA *Soup*

All the flavor of traditional lasagna is here in a hearty, comforting soup made with mafalda pasta, beef, diced tomatoes, and seasoning—plus it's topped with mozzarella cheese.

INGREDIENTS

- 1 pound ground beef
- 2 (14.5-ounce) cans garlic-roasted diced tomatoes, not drained
- 1 (24-ounce) jar marinara sauce
- 2 cups low-sodium beef broth
- 1 cup water
- 1 teaspoon dried Italian seasoning
- 8 ounces uncooked mafalda pasta (see Julie's Notes)
- 1 cup shredded mozzarella cheese

INSTRUCTIONS

1. In a large stockpot, cook the ground beef over medium-high heat for 5 to 7 minutes, until cooked through. Drain the grease.
2. Add the canned tomatoes, marinara sauce, broth, water, and Italian seasoning. Bring to a boil. Reduce the heat and simmer for 15 minutes.
3. Meanwhile, prepare the pasta according to package directions until al dente and drain.
4. Stir in the cooked pasta and simmer for 5 minutes. Serve with mozzarella cheese sprinkled on top.

JULIE'S *Notes*

If you can't find mafalda pasta, which looks like tiny lasagna noodles, broken-up lasagna noodles will also work, or any large pasta like rigatoni, penne, or farfalle.

Serve with Cheesy Garlic Bread Loaf (page 55).

Scan for more tips!

108   JULIE'S EATS & TREATS COOKBOOK

CHILI

This easy chili is made with ground beef, beans, and a blend of delicious seasonings. A hearty comforting favorite on a cold winter night!

SERVES 8

PREP TIME: 10 MINS
COOK TIME: 30 MINS
TOTAL TIME: 40 MINS

INGREDIENTS

- 1 pound ground beef
- 1 white onion, diced
- 3 cloves garlic, minced
- 1 (15-ounce) can beef broth
- 1 (16-ounce) can chili beans in medium chili sauce
- 1 (14.5-ounce) can petite diced tomatoes
- 1 (8-ounce) can tomato sauce
- 2 Tablespoons tomato paste
- 2 Tablespoons chili powder
- 1 Tablespoon ground cumin
- 1 teaspoon garlic salt
- ½ teaspoon dried oregano

INSTRUCTIONS

1. In a Dutch oven or soup pot over medium heat, cook the ground beef and onion, stirring occasionally, until the onion is translucent and the ground beef is cooked through, about 5 minutes. Add the garlic during the last minute of cooking. Drain off the grease.

2. Add the broth, beans, tomatoes, tomato sauce, tomato paste, chili powder, cumin, garlic salt, and oregano to the pot and stir to combine. Bring to a low boil, then reduce the heat to low and simmer for 20 minutes, uncovered, stirring occasionally.

3. Remove the chili from stove and let sit for 5 to 10 minutes, then serve.

JULIE'S Notes

Top the chili with sour cream and shredded cheese, if you like.
Serve with Cheddar Biscuits (page 59) or Beer Bread (page 56).

Scan for more tips!

SOUPS AND STEWS

SERVES 8

PREP TIME: 10 MINS

COOK TIME: 4 HRS 15 MINS OR 8 HRS 15 MINS

TOTAL TIME: 4 HRS 25 MINS OR 8 HRS 25 MINS

Slow Cooker WHITE CHICKEN CHILI

Every bite of this white chili is bursting with flavor from the chicken, beans, green chilies, and spices. It's creamy and such a delicious way to warm yourself up.

INGREDIENTS

- 1 pound skinless boneless chicken breasts
- 1½ teaspoons ground cumin
- 1 teaspoon salt
- ½ teaspoon ground black pepper
- ½ teaspoon dried oregano
- ½ teaspoon chili powder
- ¼ teaspoon cayenne pepper
- 1 yellow onion, minced
- 3 cloves garlic, minced
- 2 (15-ounce) cans great northern beans, drained and rinsed
- 2 (4.5-ounce) cans diced green chilies
- 1 (15-ounce) can corn, drained
- 3 cups low-sodium chicken broth
- 4 ounces reduced-fat cream cheese, diced
- ½ cup half-and-half

INSTRUCTIONS

1. Place the chicken breasts in the bottom of a 6-quart slow cooker and season with the cumin, salt, pepper, oregano, chili powder, and cayenne pepper. Add the onion, garlic, beans, green chilies, corn, and chicken broth and stir to combine. Cover the slow cooker and cook on low for 8 hours, or on high for 3 to 4 hours.

2. When the cooking time is done, remove the chicken from the pot and shred it with two forks. Return it to the slow cooker and add the cream cheese and half-and-half. Stir and cook on high for 15 minutes, or until the cream cheese is melted.

3. Stir and serve with your choice of toppings (see Julie's Notes).

JULIE'S Notes

Toppings can include sliced jalapeño peppers, diced avocado, sour cream, minced fresh cilantro, tortilla strips, shredded cheese, and whatever else you like.

Serve with Cheddar Biscuits (page 59) or Beer Bread (page 56).

Scan for more tips!

Slow Cooker ENCHILADA SOUP

Here's a dump-it-and-forget-it soup that simmers all day in your slow cooker and is ready for you when you come home. The flavor is amazing. Serve it with the toppings of your choice (see Julie's Notes).

SERVES 6

PREP TIME: 10 MINS

COOK TIME: 4 OR 8 HRS

TOTAL TIME: 4 HRS 10 MINS OR 8 HRS 10 MINS

INGREDIENTS

- 1 pound skinless boneless chicken breasts
- 2 cups low-sodium chicken broth
- 1 (10-ounce) can red enchilada sauce
- 1 (14-ounce) can fire-roasted tomatoes
- 1 (15-ounce) can corn
- 1 (4.5-ounce) can diced green chilies
- 1 (15-ounce) can black beans, drained and rinsed
- 2 cloves garlic, minced
- ½ cup diced yellow onion
- 1 teaspoon ground cumin
- 1 teaspoon salt
- 1 cup shredded Mexican cheese

INSTRUCTIONS

1. Add all ingredients except the cheese to a 5-quart slow cooker and stir to combine.

2. Cook on high for 3 to 4 hours or on low for 6 to 8 hours, until the chicken is cooked to an internal temperature of 165 degrees Fahrenheit.

3. Remove the chicken from the pot, shred using two forks, and return to the soup. Stir in the cheese and heat until melted.

JULIE'S Notes

Toppings are optional but delicious. Try diced avocado, chopped fresh cilantro, sour cream, shredded cheese, tortilla chips, or whatever else you have on hand.

Serve with Cheddar Biscuits (page 59) or Beer Bread (page 56).

SERVES 6

PREP TIME: 15 MINS

COOK TIME: 4 HRS 15 MINS OR 6 HRS 15 MIN

TOTAL TIME: 4 HRS 30 MINS OR 6 HRS 30 MIN

Slow Cooker ZUPPA TOSCANA

Craving a big bowl of soup? There's tons of flavor in this soup from spicy sausage and kale in a creamy base. This copycat Olive Garden recipe of the Tuscan classic is going to be a new favorite.

INGREDIENTS

- 1 Tablespoon olive oil
- 1 pound ground spicy Italian sausage
- 1 yellow onion, minced
- 3 cloves garlic, minced
- 6 slices bacon
- 4 large Yukon gold potatoes, cut into ½-inch dice
- 4 cups low-sodium chicken broth
- 1 teaspoon salt
- ½ teaspoon ground black pepper
- 1 cup heavy cream
- 2 Tablespoons all-purpose flour
- 3 cups chopped kale

INSTRUCTIONS

1. Heat the olive oil over medium-high heat in a large skillet. Add the sausage and crumble with a spoon. Add the onion and garlic and cook until the sausage is cooked through, about 5 minutes. Remove the sausage mixture to a plate and drain off the grease.

2. Cook the bacon in the same skillet until it's crisp. Remove and chop it into small pieces.

3. Combine the sausage mixture, bacon, potatoes, broth, salt, and pepper in a 6-quart slow cooker. Cook on low for 5½ hours, or on high for 3½ hours, until the potatoes are done.

4. Whisk together the cream and flour in a small bowl. Pour the mixture into the slow cooker, then add the kale and stir to combine. Cook on high for 30 minutes, or until the soup has thickened slightly.

JULIE'S Notes

Substitute mild sausage instead of spicy if that's more to your taste.

You can use russet potatoes instead of Yukon golds.

Cornstarch is fine to replace the flour.

Serve with Cheddar Biscuits (page 59) or Beer Bread (page 56).

Scan for more tips!

116 JULIE'S EATS & TREATS COOKBOOK

Slow Cooker **BEEF STEW**

Tender juicy beef, cooked with potatoes and carrots, makes this the best beef stew. It is rich, chunky, and hearty.

PREP TIME: 15 MINS

COOK TIME: 8 OR 10 HRS

TOTAL TIME: 8 HRS 15 MINS OR 10 HRS 15 MINS

SERVES 6

INGREDIENTS

- ¼ cup all-purpose flour
- 1 teaspoon salt
- ½ teaspoon ground black pepper
- 2 pounds beef stew meat, cut into 1-inch cubes
- 1 yellow onion, diced
- 3 cloves garlic, minced
- 3 Yukon gold or red potatoes, peeled and diced
- 4 carrots, peeled and sliced
- 2 Tablespoons Worcestershire sauce
- 1 teaspoon paprika
- 2½ cups beef broth
- 1 (8-ounce) can tomato sauce
- Optional garnish: Chopped parsley

INSTRUCTIONS

1. In a gallon-size resealable plastic bag, mix together the flour, salt, and pepper. Dump in the meat and shake until it's coated.
2. Transfer the contents of the bag to a 6-quart slow cooker and stir in the rest of the ingredients.
3. Cover and cook on low for 8 to 10 hours.

JULIE'S *Notes*

Serve with Cheddar Biscuits (page 59) or Beer Bread (page 56).

Scan for more tips!

SOUPS AND STEWS

Honey Sesame Chicken, page 130

Dinners

CHICKEN
Baked Chicken Drumsticks // 122

Baked Chicken Thighs // 125

Baked Chicken Wings // 126

Baked Sweet and Sour Chicken // 129

Honey Sesame Chicken // 130

Chicken Fried Rice // 133

Sheet Pan Chicken Fajitas // 134

Creamy Chicken Enchiladas // 137

Chicken Tetrazzini // 138

Chicken Alfredo Bake // 141

Slow Cooker Bacon Ranch
   Chicken Sandwiches // 142

Slow Cooker Italian Chicken // 145

One-Pot Cajun Chicken Pasta // 146

BEEF
Baked Spaghetti // 149

Homemade Hamburger Helper // 150

Zucchini Hamburger Skillet // 153

Slow Cooker Hamburger and
   Wild Rice Casserole // 154

Mini Meatloaves // 157

Totchos // 158

Baked Tacos // 161

Beef Enchiladas // 162

One-Pot Taco Pasta // 165

One-Pot Burrito Bowl // 166

Taco Pie // 169

Hamburger Stroganoff // 170

Stuffed Pepper Casserole // 173

Baked Meatballs in Marinara Sauce // 174

Beef and Broccoli // 177

Lasagna // 178

Garlic-Butter Steak and Potatoes // 181

Sheet Pan Steak, Potatoes,
   and Asparagus // 182

Slow Cooker French Dip Sandwiches // 185

Slow Cooker Mississippi Pot Roast // 186

PORK
Stuffed Zucchini Boats // 189

Pizza Sliders // 190

One-Pot Pizza Pasta // 193

Ham and Potato Casserole // 194

Parmesan-Crusted Pork Chops // 197

Parmesan-Crusted Tilapia // 198

SEAFOOD
Parmesan-Crusted Tilapia // 198

Shrimp Boil // 201

Shrimp Pasta // 202

SERVES 4

PREP TIME: 10 MINS

COOK TIME: 45 MINS

TOTAL TIME: 55 MINS

Baked CHICKEN DRUMSTICKS

Chicken drumsticks are tossed in a delicious seasoning made with pantry staples, then baked to tender and juicy goodness. They have an amazing flavor, crispy skin, and are a hit at every dinner table.

INGREDIENTS

Nonstick cooking spray
8 chicken drumsticks (about 2 pounds)
2 Tablespoons olive oil
Optional garnish: Chopped parsley

RUB
1½ teaspoons smoked paprika
1 teaspoon onion powder
1 teaspoon sea salt
1 teaspoon garlic powder
½ teaspoon ground black pepper
¼ teaspoon chili powder

INSTRUCTIONS

1. Preheat the oven to 425 degrees Fahrenheit. Line a large baking sheet with aluminum foil and lightly spray with nonstick cooking spray.

2. Pat the drumsticks dry with paper towels. Place in a large bowl or a resealable plastic bag, add the oil, and toss to coat.

3. In a small bowl, combine all the rub ingredients. Add to the chicken and toss until coated.

4. Place the drumsticks on the baking sheet. Bake for 40 to 45 minutes, until the internal temperature is 165 degrees Fahrenheit or higher.

JULIE'S *Notes*

Serve with Tossed Salad with Italian Dressing (page 64) and Cheesy Garlic-Butter Pasta (page 83).

Scan for more tips!

122 JULIE'S EATS & TREATS COOKBOOK

Baked CHICKEN THIGHS

If you are looking for the most amazing, juicy chicken thighs with crispy skin, this is the recipe! They have so much flavor, but are made with only a few ingredients.

SERVES 6

PREP TIME: 10 MINS
COOK TIME: 45 MINS
TOTAL TIME: 55 MINS

INGREDIENTS

Nonstick cooking spray
6 bone-in, skin-on chicken thighs
2 Tablespoons olive oil
Optional garnish: Chopped parsley

RUB
1 teaspoons smoked paprika
1 teaspoon garlic powder
1 teaspoon onion powder
1 teaspoon sea salt
½ teaspoon ground black pepper
¼ teaspoon chili powder

INSTRUCTIONS

1. Preheat the oven to 400 degrees Fahrenheit. Line a baking sheet with aluminum foil or parchment paper. Spray with nonstick spray.

2. In a small bowl, combine all the rub ingredients.

3. Pat the chicken thighs dry with paper towels and thoroughly coat with the olive oil. Sprinkle the rub mixture evenly over the thighs, turning to coat both sides. Place the chicken skin side up on the baking sheet and bake for 35 to 45 minutes, until the chicken reaches an internal temperature of 165 degrees Fahrenheit.

4. If you would like to crisp up your chicken even more, turn on the broiler and broil the chicken for 1 to 2 minutes, until it has your preferred level of crispiness.

5. Let the chicken sit for 5 minutes before serving. Garnish with the parsley, if using, and serve.

JULIE'S *Notes*

Serve with Cheesy Bacon Ranch Potatoes (page 87) and Oven-Roasted Vegetables (page 91).

Scan for more tips!

DINNERS 125

SERVES 4

PREP TIME: 10 MINS

COOK TIME: 50 MINS

TOTAL TIME: 1 HR

Baked CHICKEN WINGS

Craving some wings? These crispy wings are easy to make, tender and juicy, and flavorful from a homemade rub that is out of this world. This can be an easy appetizer or a fun dinner recipe.

INGREDIENTS

Nonstick cooking spray

2 pounds chicken wings (see Julie's Notes)

1 Tablespoon olive oil

DRY RUB

2 teaspoons baking powder

1 teaspoon salt

1 teaspoon garlic powder

1 teaspoon smoked paprika

1 teaspoon onion powder

½ teaspoon ground black pepper

¼ teaspoon chili powder

INSTRUCTIONS

1. Preheat the oven to 425 degrees Fahrenheit. Line a large baking sheet with aluminum foil and lightly spray with nonstick cooking spray. Place a baking rack on top of the foil.

2. In a small bowl, combine all the rub ingredients.

3. Pat the chicken wings dry with paper towels. Place the wings in a resealable plastic bag or a large bowl. Add the oil and toss to coat the wings. Add the rub mixture and shake or stir to coat evenly.

4. Place the chicken wings on the baking rack in an even layer, making sure they don't touch. Bake for 20 minutes, flip, and bake for an additional 20 to 30 minutes, until the internal temperature of the chicken reaches 165 degrees Fahrenheit.

JULIE'S Notes

I recommend buying a party pack of chicken wings, so the wings are precut.

For dipping sauces, try ranch, BBQ, blue cheese, or whatever is your favorite.

Serve with Roasted Sweet Potatoes (page 84) and Tossed Salad with Italian Dressing (page 64).

Scan for more tips!

126   JULIE'S EATS & TREATS COOKBOOK

Baked SWEET AND SOUR CHICKEN

Make easy sweet and sour chicken at home—it's so much better than takeout.

SERVES 8

PREP TIME: 10 MINS
COOK TIME: 1 HR 5 MINS
TOTAL TIME: 1 HR 15 MINS

INGREDIENTS

- 2 pounds skinless boneless chicken breasts
- Salt and ground black pepper to taste
- ¾ cup cornstarch
- 3 eggs, lightly beaten
- ¼ cup canola oil
- ¾ cup white granulated sugar
- ¼ cup ketchup
- ½ cup white vinegar
- 1 Tablespoon soy sauce
- 1 teaspoon garlic salt

INSTRUCTIONS

1. Preheat the oven to 325 degrees Fahrenheit. Lightly spray a 9-x-13-inch baking dish with nonstick cooking spray.

2. Pat the chicken breasts dry with paper towels. Cut the chicken into chunks and season with salt and pepper.

3. Place the cornstarch in a small bowl and the beaten eggs in another small bowl. Dip the pieces of chicken into the cornstarch to coat, then dip them into the eggs. Place on a clean plate.

4. Heat the oil in a large skillet over medium heat. Add the chicken pieces and cook, turning occasionally, until browned but not cooked through, 4 to 5 minutes. Transfer the chicken pieces to the baking dish.

5. In a small bowl, whisk together the sugar, ketchup, vinegar, soy sauce, and garlic salt. Pour the sauce over the chicken and toss to coat. Bake, stirring every 15 minutes, for 1 hour.

JULIE'S *Notes*

Serve with Fried Rice (page 79) or egg rolls for a meal.

Scan for more tips!

DINNERS 129

SERVES 4

PREP TIME: 15 MINS

COOK TIME: 15 MINS

TOTAL TIME: 30 MINS

Honey SESAME CHICKEN

Crispy pieces of chicken are tossed in a sweet, thick honey sesame sauce for a delicious Chinese-style dinner at home.

INGREDIENTS

1½ pounds skinless boneless chicken breasts, cut into 1-inch cubes

½ teaspoon salt

½ teaspoon ground black pepper

½ cup all-purpose flour

¼ cup cornstarch

½ cup vegetable oil

Optional garnish: Sliced green onions

HONEY SAUCE

3 Tablespoons ketchup

2 Tablespoons honey

1 Tablespoon low-sodium soy sauce

1 Tablespoon sesame oil

1 Tablespoon rice wine vinegar

2 Tablespoons brown sugar

2 cloves garlic, minced

1 Tablespoon sesame seeds, for garnish

INSTRUCTIONS

1. Place the chicken breast cubes in a large bowl and season with the salt and pepper.

2. In a small bowl, whisk together the flour and cornstarch. Add to the chicken and toss until the chicken is coated, but do not overmix.

3. Heat the vegetable oil in a large nonstick skillet or wok over medium-high heat. Carefully lower the coated chicken into the oil, making sure to spread the chicken apart in the pan so the pieces don't touch. Fry, turning occasionally, until golden and crispy brown on all sides, 6 to 8 minutes total. Transfer the chicken to a plate lined with paper towels.

4. Meanwhile, in a small bowl, whisk together all the honey sauce ingredients.

5. Add the sauce mixture to a large saucepan and bring to a boil over medium-high heat. Reduce the heat and simmer for 2 to 3 minutes, until the sauce has thickened. Add the cooked chicken and mix until coated.

6. Transfer the chicken to a serving bowl, top with the sesame seeds, and serve immediately.

JULIE'S *Notes*

We like to serve this over cooked white rice.

Chicken FRIED RICE

SERVES 4

PREP TIME: 10 MINS
COOK TIME: 10 MINS
TOTAL TIME: 20 MINS

Use up leftover rice and chicken to make a quick and easy one-pan dinner. It's so easy and full of flavor—even better than takeout.

INGREDIENTS

- 2 Tablespoons sesame oil
- 2 Tablespoons canola or vegetable oil
- ½ cup diced yellow onion
- 2 cups frozen peas and carrots
- 1½ teaspoons minced garlic
- 4 cups cooked white rice, cold
- 1 pound cooked chicken, cut into ½-inch cubes (about 2 cups)
- 3 eggs, lightly beaten
- ¼ cup soy sauce
- Salt and ground black pepper to taste
- Optional garnish: Sliced green onions

INSTRUCTIONS

1. Heat the sesame and canola oils in a large wok or frying pan over medium heat. Add the yellow onion and peas and carrots and sauté until the onion is translucent. Add the garlic and cook for about 1 minute, until fragrant. Add the cooked rice and chicken and stir to combine.

2. Push the mixture to the side of the pan. Pour the eggs into the empty side of the pan and scramble with a spatula. When the eggs are fully cooked, combine them with the rice.

3. Add the soy sauce and stir to mix. Season with salt and pepper and garnish with the green onions, if desired. Serve immediately.

JULIE'S Notes

You can easily substitute cooked beef (cubes of steak or even ground beef), cooked ground pork, or diced ham for the cooked chicken.

Scan for more tips!

DINNERS 133

SERVES 5

PREP TIME: 20 MINS

COOK TIME: 25 MINS

TOTAL TIME: 45 MINS

Sheet Pan CHICKEN FAJITAS

Dinner does not get easier than these fajitas made on a baking sheet. Seasoned and roasted chicken and vegetables are served in a warm tortilla.

INGREDIENTS

FAJITA SEASONING

2 teaspoons chili powder

1½ teaspoons ground cumin

1½ teaspoons smoked paprika

½ teaspoon onion powder

½ teaspoon garlic powder

½ teaspoon salt

¼ teaspoon dried oregano

¼ teaspoon ground black pepper

3 Tablespoons olive oil

FAJITAS

Nonstick cooking spray

1½ pounds boneless, skinless chicken breasts, cut into thin stripes

1 red bell pepper, cut into thin strips

1 yellow bell pepper, cut into thin strips

1 red onion, cut into wedges

3 cloves garlic, minced

8 to 10 (8-inch) flour or corn tortillas, warmed

¼ cup chopped fresh cilantro leaves

1 lime, juiced

INSTRUCTIONS

1. Make the fajita seasoning: In a small bowl, combine the chili powder, cumin, paprika, onion powder, garlic powder, salt, oregano, and pepper. Add the olive oil to the bowl and stir to combine.

2. To make the fajitas, preheat the oven to 425 degrees Fahrenheit. Lightly spray a large baking sheet with nonstick cooking spray.

3. Arrange the chicken, red and yellow bell peppers, onion, and garlic in a single layer on the baking sheet. Pour the fajita seasoning on top and gently toss to combine.

4. Bake for 20 to 25 minutes, until the chicken is completely cooked through and the vegetables are crisp-tender.

5. Wrap the tortillas in aluminum foil and place in the oven during the last 5 minutes of cooking.

6. Garnish the chicken fajita mixture with the chopped cilantro, drizzle lime juice over everything, and mix. Serve the fajita mixture in the warm tortillas, with optional toppings (see Julie's Notes), if desired.

JULIE'S Notes

For fajita toppings, try sour cream, sliced avocado, gua-camole, pico de gallo, and/or shredded cheese.

Serve with Spanish Rice (page 80).

Creamy CHICKEN ENCHILADAS

SERVES 5

PREP TIME: 20 MINS
COOK TIME: 45 MINS
TOTAL TIME: 1 HR 5 MINS

Soft flour tortillas are filled with a chicken and cream cheese mixture, then topped with seasoned sour cream and baked. Don't forget the melted cheddar on top!

INGREDIENTS

- Nonstick cooking spray
- 4 ounces cream cheese, softened
- 1 Tablespoon water
- 1 teaspoon onion powder
- 1 teaspoon ground cumin
- ¼ teaspoon salt
- ⅛ teaspoon ground black pepper
- 2½ cups diced cooked chicken
- 10 (6-inch) flour tortillas, room temperature
- 1 (10¾-ounce) can condensed cream of chicken soup
- 1 cup sour cream
- 1 (4-ounce) can chopped green chilies
- 1 cup shredded cheddar cheese

INSTRUCTIONS

1. Preheat the oven to 350 degrees Fahrenheit. Lightly spray a 13-x-9-inch baking dish with nonstick cooking spray.

2. In a large bowl, beat the cream cheese, water, onion powder, cumin, salt, and pepper until smooth. Stir in the chicken. Spoon ¼ cup of the chicken mixture down the center of each tortilla. Roll them up and place seam side down in the baking dish.

3. In a medium bowl, combine the soup, sour cream, and chilies and pour over the enchiladas.

4. Bake, uncovered, for 30 to 40 minutes, until everything is heated through. Sprinkle with cheddar cheese and bake 5 minutes longer, until the cheese is melted.

JULIE'S Notes

Serve with Spanish Rice (page 80).

To prepare these in advance, make the enchiladas through Step 3. Cover the pan with a lid, aluminum foil, or plastic wrap and refrigerate up to 24 hours. To serve, let the pan sit out on the counter while the oven preheats. Then bake according to the directions, but plan on about 10 minutes of extra bake time because the enchiladas are cold.

To freeze this recipe, prepare through step 3. Cover tightly with plastic wrap and then foil or a lid and freeze for up to 3 months. The night before you want to serve, transfer the pan to the refrigerator to thaw overnight. Then bake according to the directions in the note above.

Scan for more tips!

DINNERS

SERVES 8

PREP TIME: 15 MINS

COOK TIME: 30 MINS

TOTAL TIME: 45 MINS

JULIE'S Notes

Before baking, we like to split this into two 8-x-8-inch pans and freeze one, because it makes so much. To freeze the unbaked casserole, cover with foil, then the baking dish lid (or place in a resealable freezer bag) and freeze for up to 3 months. Thaw overnight in the refrigerator and bake according to directions, adding 5 to 10 minutes to baking time.

Substitute 2 (12.5-ounce each) cans shredded chicken for the cooked chicken breast.

Serve with Oven-Roasted Vegetables (page 91) or Tossed Salad with Italian Dressing (page 64).

Chicken TETRAZZINI

You can't beat a classic like this creamy, cheesy, delicious tetrazzini. Chicken and pasta tossed in a creamy sauce with tons of flavor make a classic comfort food that the entire family will love for dinner.

INGREDIENTS

- Nonstick cooking spray
- ½ cup salted butter, softened
- 2 cups (about 1 pound) cooked chicken
- 1 (10.5-ounce) can condensed cream of chicken soup
- 1 (10.5-ounce) can condensed cream of mushroom soup
- 16 ounces sour cream
- 1½ cups frozen green peas
- ½ cup chicken broth
- 1 teaspoon salt
- ½ teaspoon ground black pepper
- ½ teaspoon garlic powder
- 1 pound linguine, cooked
- 2 cups shredded mozzarella cheese
- Optional garnish: Chopped parsley

INSTRUCTIONS

1. Preheat the oven to 350 degrees Fahrenheit. Lightly spray a 9-x-13-inch baking dish with nonstick cooking spray.

2. Combine the butter, cooked chicken, both cans of soup, the sour cream, peas, chicken broth, salt, pepper, and garlic powder in a large bowl. Stir until combined.

3. Add the noodles to the chicken mixture and stir until combined.

4. Pour the noodle mixture into the baking dish and sprinkle the mozzarella cheese on top. Bake for 25 to 30 minutes, until it's warmed through and the cheese is melted and is turning slightly golden brown on top. Sprinkle with the parsley, if you like, and serve.

Scan for more tips!

SERVES 6

CHICKEN ALFREDO *Bake*

Delicious creamy homemade Alfredo sauce is perfect baked with chicken and pasta for a hearty casserole.

PREP TIME: 15 MINS

COOK TIME: 30 MINS

TOTAL TIME: 45 MINS

INGREDIENTS

ALFREDO SAUCE

2 cups heavy cream

½ cup salted butter, cut into large cubes

4 cloves garlic, minced

½ teaspoon garlic powder

½ teaspoon dried Italian seasoning

½ teaspoon salt

¼ teaspoon ground black pepper

1 cup grated parmesan cheese

CHICKEN BAKE

Nonstick cooking spray

1 pound penne pasta, cooked according to the package directions

3 cups cooked chicken

2 cups shredded mozzarella cheese

Optional garnish: Chopped parsley

INSTRUCTIONS

1. Preheat the oven to 375 degrees Fahrenheit.

2. To make the sauce, heat the cream and butter in a medium saucepan or skillet over medium-low heat, whisking until the butter is completely melted. Add the garlic, garlic powder, Italian seasoning, salt, and pepper and whisk until combined. Bring to a gentle simmer, making sure not to boil it, and cook, whisking constantly, for 3 to 4 minutes, until the sauce starts to thicken. Stir in the parmesan cheese and whisk until melted. Remove from the heat.

3. Spray a 9-x-13-inch baking dish with nonstick cooking spray. Combine the cooked pasta and cooked chicken in a large bowl. Pour the Alfredo sauce over the top and stir until coated.

4. Pour the pasta mixture into the baking pan and top with the mozzarella cheese. Bake, uncovered, for 20 minutes, or until the pasta is bubbly and the cheese has just started to brown.

JULIE'S *Notes*

You can use two (15-ounce) jars of Alfredo sauce instead of making your own.

And you can substitute 2 (12.5-ounce each) cans canned chicken breast for the diced cooked chicken breast

Serve with Cheesy Garlic Bread Loaf (page 55) or Tossed Salad with Italian Dressing (page 64).

SERVES 6

PREP TIME: 10 MINS

COOK TIME: 4 HRS 15 MINS OR 8 HRS 15 MINS

TOTAL TIME: 4 HRS 25 MINS OR 8 HRS 25 MINS

Slow Cooker BACON RANCH CHICKEN SANDWICHES

Here are delicious, irresistible sandwiches of shredded chicken and cream cheese combined with ranch seasoning, cheddar cheese, and bacon. It's made in your slow cooker and is the perfect easy-to-make sandwich filling for busy weeknight meals or quick lunches.

INGREDIENTS

- Nonstick cooking spray
- 2 pounds skinless boneless chicken breasts
- 1 (1-ounce) package ranch seasoning mix
- 2 (8-ounce) packages cream cheese, cubed
- 1 cup shredded cheddar cheese
- 1 (2.8-ounce) package Hormel real bacon bits
- Buns for serving

INSTRUCTIONS

1. Spray a 6-quart slow cooker with nonstick cooking spray. Place the chicken breasts in the bottom of the slow cooker and sprinkle on the ranch seasoning and cream cheese.
2. Cover and cook on low for 6 to 8 hours, or on high for 4 hours.
3. Shred the chicken right in the cooker using two forks. Add the cheese and bacon bits and stir to combine. Cook on low for 10 to 15 minutes, until the cheese is melted.
4. Serve on buns.

JULIE'S Notes

We like to serve this over pasta to change things up!

Serve with Oven-Roasted Vegetables (page 91).

Scan for more tips!

142 JULIE'S EATS & TREATS COOKBOOK

Slow Cooker ITALIAN CHICKEN

This easy slow cooker recipe has a ton of flavor. It's a family favorite and one of the easiest dinners to make, with hardly any prep work.

SERVES 6

PREP TIME: 10 MINS
COOK TIME: 4 OR 6 HRS
TOTAL TIME: 4 HRS 10 MINS OR 6 HRS 10 MINS

INGREDIENTS

- Nonstick cooking spray
- 4 skinless boneless chicken breasts
- ½ teaspoon ground black pepper
- 2 (10.5-ounce) cans condensed cream of chicken soup
- 8 ounces cream cheese, cubed, room temperature
- 1 (0.6-ounce) package zesty Italian salad dressing mix

INSTRUCTIONS

1. Spray a 6-quart slow cooker with nonstick cooking spray. Place the chicken in the slow cooker and season with the pepper.

2. In a small bowl, combine the soup, cream cheese, and Italian dressing mix. Pour over the chicken.

3. Cover and cook on low for 5 to 6 hours, or on high for 4 hours.

4. When the cooking time is up, carefully shred the chicken with two forks and mix it up into the gravy in the slow cooker.

JULIE'S Notes

We love serving this over wide egg noodles or rice to make it a meal. Serve with Tossed Salad with Italian Dressing (page 64).

Scan for more tips!

DINNERS 145

SERVES 6

PREP TIME: 10 MINS
COOK TIME: 30 MINS
TOTAL TIME: 40 MINS

One-Pot CAJUN CHICKEN PASTA

This amazing, creamy Cajun pasta is made in one pot for a quick and easy dinner. It combines a creamy sauce, penne pasta, and chicken with the perfect amount of Cajun spice.

INGREDIENTS

- 1 pound skinless boneless chicken breasts, cut into chunks
- 1 Tablespoon Cajun seasoning, plus more for garnish
- 2 Tablespoons extra-virgin olive oil
- ½ cup diced yellow onion
- 4 cloves garlic, minced
- 4 cups chicken broth
- 2½ cups heavy cream
- 1 pound uncooked penne pasta
- ½ cup grated parmesan cheese
- 2 Roma tomatoes, seeded and diced, for garnish
- Chopped fresh parsley, for garnish

INSTRUCTIONS

1. In a large skillet, toss the chicken, Cajun seasoning and olive oil together. Add the onion and cook over medium heat, stirring to sear the chicken, for about 5 minutes, until the onion is translucent. Stir in the garlic and cook for 1 minute more.

2. Add the chicken broth, cream, and pasta. Turn the heat to high, bring to a boil, then turn the heat to low. Cover and simmer for 15 minutes, or until the pasta is tender. Stir in the parmesan cheese.

3. To serve, top the pasta with the tomatoes, parsley, and additional Cajun seasoning to taste.

JULIE'S Notes

Serve with Oven-Roasted Vegetables (page 91) or Tossed Salad with Italian Dressing (page 64).

Scan for more tips!

Baked **SPAGHETTI**

This comforting pasta bake has layers of spaghetti, ground beef, marinara, and, of course, cheese.

SERVES 8

PREP TIME: 15 MINS

COOK TIME: 50 MINS

TOTAL TIME: 1 HR 5 MINS

INGREDIENTS

Nonstick cooking spray

1 pound uncooked spaghetti

1 pound ground beef

1 yellow onion, chopped

1 (24-ounce) jar marinara sauce

1 teaspoon dried Italian seasoning

2 eggs

⅓ cup grated parmesan cheese

3 Tablespoons salted butter, melted

16 ounces cottage cheese, divided

3 cups shredded mozzarella cheese, divided

INSTRUCTIONS

1. Preheat the oven to 350 degrees Fahrenheit. Lightly spray a 9-x-13-inch baking dish with nonstick cooking spray.

2. Cook the spaghetti according to the directions on the package until al dente, then drain.

3. While the pasta is cooking, heat a large skillet over medium heat. Add the ground beef and onion and cook and stir until the meat is browned and the onion is soft and translucent, 5 to 7 minutes. Drain the grease from the pan. Stir in the marinara sauce and Italian seasoning.

4. In a large bowl, whisk the eggs, parmesan cheese, and melted butter. Add the drained spaghetti and toss to coat.

5. Spread half the spaghetti mixture in the baking dish. Top with 1 cup of the cottage cheese, 1 cup of the mozzarella cheese, and half of the meat sauce. Repeat the layers with the rest of the spaghetti mixture, remaining 1 cup cottage cheese, 1 cup of the remaining mozzarella, and the remaining meat sauce.

6. Cover the pan with aluminum foil. Bake for 40 minutes. Remove the foil and sprinkle the remaining 1 cup mozzarella cheese on top. Bake until the cheese is melted and lightly browned, about 5 minutes.

JULIE'S *Notes*

Serve with Tossed Salad with Italian Dressing (page 64) and Cheesy Garlic Bread Loaf (page 55).

SERVES 6

PREP TIME: 10 MINS
COOK TIME: 30 MINS
TOTAL TIME: 40 MINS

Homemade HAMBURGER HELPER

This one-pot recipe is a cheesy, rich, and delicious mix of ground beef, macaroni, and cheddar—and better than your childhood favorite from a box.

INGREDIENTS

- 1 pound ground beef
- ½ cup diced yellow onion
- 1 Tablespoon minced garlic
- 2 Tablespoons tomato paste
- 2 teaspoons Worcestershire sauce
- ½ teaspoon salt
- ½ teaspoon ground black pepper
- 4 cups low-sodium beef broth
- 1 cup water
- 1 pound uncooked elbow macaroni
- 1 cup shredded cheddar cheese

INSTRUCTIONS

1. In a large skillet or Dutch oven, cook the ground beef and onion over medium-high heat for 5 to 7 minutes, until the beef is cooked through. During the last minute of cooking, add the garlic. Drain off the grease.

2. Reduce the heat to low and add the tomato paste, Worcestershire sauce, salt, and pepper. Stir until combined.

3. Add the broth, water, and macaroni. Stir to combine. Turn the heat to medium and bring to a boil. Cover the pan, reduce the heat to low, and simmer for 12 to 15 minutes, until the macaroni is cooked through.

4. Remove the pan from the heat and stir in the cheese. Cover and give it a few minutes to let the cheese melt.

JULIE'S Notes

Serve with Oven-Roasted Vegetables (page 91).

Scan for more tips!

ZUCCHINI HAMBURGER *Skillet*

SERVES 4

PREP TIME: 10 MINS
COOK TIME: 25 MINS
TOTAL TIME: 35 MINS

Here's a delicious one-pot dinner that is light and healthy. It has ground beef, brown rice, zucchini, green pepper, and tomatoes, and you can have it on the dinner table in 35 minutes.

INGREDIENTS

- 1 pound ground beef
- 1 medium yellow onion, chopped
- 1 small green bell pepper, chopped
- 3 cloves garlic, minced
- 2 teaspoons chili powder
- ¾ teaspoon salt
- ¼ teaspoon ground black pepper
- 3 medium zucchini, cubed
- 2 Roma tomatoes, seeded and diced
- ¼ cup water
- 1 cup uncooked instant brown rice
- 1 cup shredded Colby jack cheese

INSTRUCTIONS

1. In a large skillet over medium-high heat, cook the ground beef with the onion and bell pepper until the meat is no longer pink, 5 to 7 minutes. Drain off the grease.

2. Stir in the garlic, chili powder, salt, pepper, zucchini, tomatoes, water, and rice. Bring to a boil. Reduce the heat, cover, and simmer until the rice is tender, 10 to 15 minutes.

3. Sprinkle in the cheese. Remove the pan from the heat and let stand until the cheese is melted.

JULIE'S *Notes*

As the zucchini cooks, it releases water, so you don't need much water for the rice. With that being said, every zucchini has a different water content. If the mix is looking a little dry in step 2, add a little more water.

Scan for more tips!

DINNERS 153

SERVES 6

PREP TIME: 20 MINS

COOK TIME: 4 HRS

TOTAL TIME: 4 HRS 20 MINS

Slow Cooker HAMBURGER AND WILD RICE CASSEROLE

This is a true Minnesota hot dish recipe that my sister-in-law shared with me. It's a mixture of ground beef, celery, wild rice, soy sauce, and mushrooms that my kids request all the time.

INGREDIENTS

1½ pounds ground beef

1 small yellow onion, diced

1½ cups chopped celery

1 (6-ounce) box Ben's Original long grain and wild rice, original recipe

1 (10.5-ounce) can condensed cream of mushroom soup

1 (10.5-ounce) can condensed chicken with rice soup

1 (8-ounce) can mushroom pieces and stems, drained

1 cup water

2 Tablespoons soy sauce

INSTRUCTIONS

1. In a large skillet, cook the ground beef, onion, and celery over medium-high heat for 5 to 7 minutes, until the meat is cooked through. Drain off the grease.

2. Transfer to a 6-quart slow cooker, add all the remaining ingredients, and stir to combine. Cook for 4 hours on low.

JULIE'S Notes

You can also bake this in a 9-x-13-inch casserole dish at 350 degrees Fahrenheit for 1½ hours.

Serve with Cheddar Biscuits (page 59) or Oven-Roasted Vegetables (page 91).

Mini **MEATLOAVES**

These individual servings of cheesy meatloaf topped with a delicious sweet sauce were a frequent dinner when I was growing up—and now I make it regularly for my family.

SERVES 8

PREP TIME: 15 MINS
COOK TIME: 45 MINS
TOTAL TIME: 1 HR

INGREDIENTS

- Nonstick cooking spray
- 1 egg
- ¾ cup milk
- 1 cup shredded cheddar cheese
- ½ cup quick rolled oats
- ½ cup chopped yellow onion
- 1 teaspoon salt
- 1 pound lean ground beef
- ½ cup ketchup
- ⅓ cup packed brown sugar
- 1 teaspoon mustard
- Optional garnish: Chopped parsley

INSTRUCTIONS

1. Preheat the oven to 350 degrees Fahrenheit. Lightly spray a 13-x-9-inch baking dish with nonstick cooking spray.

2. In a large bowl, beat the egg and milk. Stir in the cheese, oats, onion, and salt. Add the beef and mix well.

3. Shape the mixture into eight loaves and arrange in the baking dish.

4. In a small bowl, combine the ketchup, brown sugar, and mustard. Spoon the sauce over the loaves. Bake, uncovered, for 45 minutes, or until the meat is no longer pink.

JULIE'S *Notes*

Serve with Bacon-Wrapped Green Beans (page 92) and Cheesy Bacon Ranch Potatoes (page 87).

Scan for more tips!

DINNERS 157

SERVES 6

PREP TIME: 10 MINS

COOK TIME: 30 MINS

TOTAL TIME: 40 MINS

TOTCHOS

Everyone's going to love Tater Tot nachos! Crispy, seasoned Tater Tots are topped with taco meat, black beans, cheese, corn, and more for a fun dinner.

INGREDIENTS

1 (28-ounce) package frozen Tater Tots

1 (1-ounce) package taco seasoning

1 pound ground beef

1 (15-ounce) jar nacho cheese sauce

1 (15-ounce) can black beans, drained and rinsed

1 (15.25-ounce) can corn, drained

1½ cups shredded cheddar cheese

½ cup Hormel real bacon bits

1 cup diced tomatoes

INSTRUCTIONS

1. Toss the Tater Tots with half the taco seasoning, then spread them out on a large baking sheet. Bake as directed on the package (usually 20 to 24 minutes at 450 degrees Fahrenheit). Leave the oven on when they're done but reduce the temperature to 350 degrees Fahrenheit.

2. While the tots are baking, heat a large skillet over medium heat. Add the ground beef and the remaining taco seasoning and cook until no pink remains, 5 to 7 minutes, using a spatula to break the meat up as you go.

3. Remove the Tater Tots from the oven and top with the ground beef mixture, nacho cheese sauce, black beans, corn, cheddar cheese, and bacon bits.

4. Return the Tater Tots to the oven to bake at 350 degrees Fahrenheit for 10 minutes, or until the cheese is melted and the topping is warmed through.

5. Remove the totchos and add the diced tomatoes and any additional desired toppings (see Julie's Notes). Serve immediately.

JULIE'S Notes

Add your favorite toppings: Diced red onions, sliced green onions, sliced black olives, shredded iceberg lettuce, guacamole, cut limes, cilantro, sliced jalapeños, and sour cream are all great options.

Baked **TACOS**

These baked tacos are so easy to make for dinner, and everyone can customize them with their own toppings. You can't beat a 30-minute meal!

SERVES 5

PREP TIME: 10 MINS

COOK TIME: 20 MINS

TOTAL TIME: 30 MINS

INGREDIENTS

Nonstick cooking spray

1 Tablespoon olive oil

1 pound ground beef

1 medium yellow onion, diced

2 cloves garlic, minced

1 (1-ounce) package taco seasoning

1 cup chunky salsa

1 (10-count) package Old El Paso Stand 'n Stuff taco shells

¾ cup canned refried beans

1½ cups shredded Mexican cheese

INSTRUCTIONS

1. Preheat the oven to 400 degrees Fahrenheit. Spray a 9-x-13-inch baking dish with nonstick cooking spray.

2. In a large skillet, heat the oil over medium-high heat. Add the ground beef, onion, and garlic and cook until the meat is browned, 5 to 7 minutes. Drain off the grease.

3. Stir in the taco seasoning and salsa. Lower the heat and simmer for 3 to 5 minutes.

4. Line up the taco shells in the baking dish. Fill each one with refried beans, then the taco meat and shredded cheese. Bake for 8 to 10 minutes, or until the cheese is melted.

5. Serve immediately with your favorite taco toppings (see Julie's Notes).

JULIE'S Notes

Try these taco toppings: shredded lettuce, diced tomatoes, sour cream, guacamole, pico de gallo, hot sauce, sliced jalapeños, cut limes, and sliced olives.

Serve with Spanish Rice (page 80) on the side.

SERVES 5

PREP TIME: 15 MINS
COOK TIME: 35 MINS
TOTAL TIME: 50 MINS

Beef ENCHILADAS

Soft tortillas are filled with ground beef, cheese, and green chilies, then covered with enchilada sauce and more cheese. It's quick, easy, and delicious.

INGREDIENTS

- Nonstick cooking spray
- 1 pound ground beef
- 1 (19-ounce) can red enchilada sauce, divided
- 1 (4.5-ounce) can chopped green chilies
- 10 (6-inch) flour tortillas
- 2 cups shredded cheddar cheese

INSTRUCTIONS

1. Preheat the oven to 375 degrees Fahrenheit. Spray a 13-x-9-inch baking dish with nonstick cooking spray.
2. In a large skillet, cook the ground beef over medium-high heat for 5 to 7 minutes, until cooked through. Drain the grease. Stir ½ cup of the enchilada sauce and the whole can of chopped green chilies into the browned beef.
3. Spread ½ cup of the enchilada sauce evenly in the bottom of the baking dish.
4. Spread ¼ cup of the beef mixture down the center of each tortilla, then sprinkle each with about 1 Tablespoon of cheese. Wrap the tortillas tightly around the filling. Place seam side down in the baking dish. Top the whole thing with the remaining enchilada sauce and sprinkle with the remaining cheese.
5. Bake for 20 to 25 minutes, until hot and bubbly. Let sit for 5 minutes before serving.

JULIE'S Notes

Serve with Spanish Rice (page 80).

Scan for more tips!

One-Pot **TACO PASTA**

SERVES 4

PREP TIME: 10 MINS

COOK TIME: 30 MINS

TOTAL TIME: 40 MINS

This easy one-pot dinner is a delicious combo of pasta shells, taco meat, and cheese.

INGREDIENTS

1 pound ground beef

2 cloves garlic, minced

2 cups beef broth

1 (14.5-ounce) can petite diced tomatoes

1 cup milk

2 Tablespoons tomato paste

1 (1-ounce) package taco seasoning

8 ounces uncooked medium pasta shells

½ cup shredded cheddar cheese

4 ounces Velveeta cheese, cut into cubes

Optional garnish: Chopped parsley

INSTRUCTIONS

1. In a large skillet or Dutch oven, cook the ground beef over medium-high heat for 5 to 7 minutes, until cooked through. When the cooking time is almost done, add the garlic and sauté for 1 minute, or until fragrant. Drain the grease.

2. Add the beef broth, tomatoes, milk, tomato paste, and taco seasoning to the skillet and stir to combine. Bring to a gentle boil and stir in the pasta.

3. Cover and cook for 14 to 15 minutes, stirring occasionally, until the pasta is cooked al dente.

4. Remove the cover, turn the heat to low, and gradually stir in the cheddar cheese and Velveeta until both are melted.

5. Remove from the heat, let stand for 5 minutes, and garnish with the parsley, if using.

JULIE'S Notes

If you want more heat, substitute a (10-ounce) can of Ro*Tel diced tomatoes and green chilies for the petite diced tomatoes.

SERVES 6

PREP TIME: 15 MINS

COOK TIME: 30 MINS

TOTAL TIME: 45 MINS

One-Pot BURRITO BOWL

This burrito bowl has so much flavor from ground beef, peppers, black beans, corn, and taco seasoning. It's an easy and delicious one-pot meal.

INGREDIENTS

1 Tablespoon olive oil

1 pound lean ground beef

½ cup diced yellow onion

½ cup diced red bell pepper

½ cup salsa

1 (15-ounce) can black beans, drained and rinsed

1 (15-ounce) can corn, drained

1 (14.5-ounce) can Ro*Tel diced tomatoes and green chilies

1 cup uncooked white rice

1 (1-ounce) package taco seasoning

½ teaspoon chili powder

2 cups low-sodium beef broth

1 cup shredded Mexican cheese

INSTRUCTIONS

1. In a large skillet, heat the olive oil over medium heat. Add the ground beef, onion, and bell pepper and cook until the beef is browned, 5 to 7 minutes. Drain off the grease.

2. Stir in the salsa, black beans, corn, Ro*Tel, rice, taco seasoning, and chili powder. Pour in the beef broth and bring to a boil. Reduce the heat, cover, and simmer for 15 minutes, or until the rice is completely cooked.

3. Sprinkle the cheese on top, cover the skillet, and remove from the heat. Let it sit for 5 minutes, or until the cheese is melted, then serve with toppings of choice (see Julie's Notes).

JULIE'S Notes

Serve with your favorite toppings, such as sour cream, chopped cilantro, green onions, tomatoes, guacamole, sliced avocado, jalapeño peppers, or hot sauce.

We like to serve this over lettuce in salad bowls and offer tortilla chips on the side.

TACO *Pie*

SERVES 6

PREP TIME: 15 MINS
COOK TIME: 35 MINS
TOTAL TIME: 50 MINS

A crust of crescent rolls is piled high with seasoned ground beef, sour cream, cheese, and nacho cheese chips. This dish was a favorite of my siblings when we were growing up, and now my kids love it too.

INGREDIENTS

- Nonstick cooking spray
- 1 pound ground beef
- 1 (1-ounce) package taco seasoning
- ½ cup water
- 1 (8-ounce) tube crescent rolls
- 1 cup sour cream
- 1 cup shredded cheddar cheese
- 1 cup crushed nacho cheese tortilla chips

INSTRUCTIONS

1. Preheat the oven to 350 degrees Fahrenheit. Lightly spray a 9-inch pie plate with nonstick cooking spray.

2. In a large skillet, cook the ground beef over medium-high heat for 5 to 7 minutes, until cooked through. Drain off the grease. Add the taco seasoning and water and simmer for 5 minutes.

3. Unroll the crescent rolls and line the pie plate with them. Use your fingers to flatten the dough to cover the bottom and press it up the sides to form a pie shell. Add the ground beef mixture, then the sour cream, then the cheese, and top with the crushed chips.

4. Bake for 25 minutes, or until the crust is golden brown and the cheese is melted.

Scan for more tips!

DINNERS 169

SERVES 6

PREP TIME: 10 MINS
COOK TIME: 20 MINS
TOTAL TIME: 30 MINS

Hamburger STROGANOFF

Creamy ground beef in a sour cream sauce is spooned over egg noodles for a hearty classic dinner.

INGREDIENTS

- 1 (16-ounce) package uncooked egg noodles
- ¼ cup salted butter
- ½ cup minced yellow onion
- 1 clove garlic, minced
- 1 pound ground beef
- 2 Tablespoons all-purpose flour
- 1 teaspoon salt
- ¼ teaspoon ground black pepper
- 1 (8-ounce) can sliced mushrooms, drained; or 8 ounces sliced fresh mushrooms
- 1 (10.5-ounce) can condensed cream of mushroom or cream of chicken soup
- 1 cup sour cream

INSTRUCTIONS

1. Prepare the egg noodles according to package directions and drain.
2. Meanwhile, in a large skillet, melt the butter over medium-high heat. Add the onion and sauté until translucent. Add the garlic and sauté for 1 minute, or until fragrant. Stir in the ground beef and cook over medium-high heat for 5 to 7 minutes, until browned.
3. Stir in the flour, salt, and pepper, then the mushrooms and mix. Turn down the heat and cook for 5 minutes. Drain off the grease.
4. Add the soup to the skillet and simmer, uncovered, for 10 minutes. Remove from the heat, mix in the sour cream, and stir to completely combine.
5. Serve over the prepared egg noodles.

JULIE'S Notes

Change it up by serving the hamburger mixture over mashed potatoes or rice instead of egg noodles.

Serve with Oven-Roasted Vegetables (page 91) or Tossed Salad with Italian Dressing (page 64).

Scan for more tips!

170 JULIE'S EATS & TREATS COOKBOOK

SERVES 6

Stuffed PEPPER CASSEROLE

Skip the fuss of stuffed peppers and make this delicious casserole that has all the flavor. It's cheesy and beefy, with peppers that don't have to be stuffed.

PREP TIME: 15 MINS

COOK TIME: 1 HR 10 MINS

TOTAL TIME: 1 HR 25 MINS

INGREDIENTS

Nonstick cooking spray

1 pound lean ground beef

2 large bell peppers, any color or a mix, diced

1 yellow onion, diced

3 cloves garlic, minced

3 Tablespoons Worcestershire sauce

1 teaspoon dried Italian seasoning

½ teaspoon salt

½ teaspoon ground black pepper

½ teaspoon smoked paprika

2 cups shredded cheddar cheese, divided

2½ cups low-sodium beef broth

1 (15-ounce) can fire-roasted diced tomatoes

1 cup uncooked long-grain white rice

INSTRUCTIONS

1. Preheat the oven to 375 degrees Fahrenheit. Spray a 9-x-13-inch casserole dish with nonstick cooking spray.

2. In a large skillet, combine the ground beef, bell peppers, and onion and cook over medium heat until the beef is cooked through, 5 to 7 minutes. Drain off the grease. Add the garlic, Worcestershire sauce, Italian seasoning, salt, pepper, and paprika and mix to combine.

3. Measure out and set aside ½ cup of shredded cheese. Add the rest of the cheese to the skillet, along with the broth, tomatoes, and rice. Stir to combine.

4. Pour the mixture into the casserole dish and top with the reserved ½ cup cheese. Cover with aluminum foil and bake until the rice is cooked through, about 1 hour.

5. Let the casserole rest 10 minutes before serving.

SERVES 6

PREP TIME: 15 MINS

COOK TIME: 45 MINS

TOTAL TIME: 1 HR

Baked MEATBALLS IN MARINARA SAUCE

Savory baked meatballs in marinara sauce are topped with melted mozzarella cheese—the combination is so tender and delicious. Serve over pasta for an easy meal.

INGREDIENTS

Nonstick cooking spray

1 (24-ounce) jar marinara sauce, divided

1½ pounds ground beef

¾ cups Italian-style bread crumbs

½ cup minced yellow onion

1 egg, lightly beaten

¼ cup grated parmesan cheese

1 Tablespoon dried parsley

1 teaspoon minced garlic

1½ teaspoons dried Italian seasoning

1 teaspoon salt

¼ teaspoon ground black pepper

2 cups shredded mozzarella cheese

Optional garnish: Chopped parsley

INSTRUCTIONS

1. Preheat the oven to 375 degrees Fahrenheit. Spray a 9-x-13-inch baking pan with nonstick cooking spray. Spread 1 cup of the marinara sauce on the bottom of the pan.

2. In a large bowl, combine the ground beef, breadcrumbs, onion, egg, parmesan cheese, parsley, garlic, Italian seasoning, salt, and pepper. Mix until just combined.

3. Shape the beef mixture into 1½-inch meatballs and place in the baking pan. Spoon the remaining marinara sauce over the meatballs. Cover the pan with aluminum foil and bake for 35 minutes, until the meatballs are cooked through and 160 degrees Fahrenheit in the center.

4. Take off the foil, top the meatballs with the mozzarella cheese, and bake for 10 more minutes, until the cheese is melted and bubbly. If desired, broil for 1 to 2 minutes to brown the cheese. Serve immediately.

JULIE'S *Notes*

We like to serve these over pasta with Tossed Salad with Italian Dressing (page 64) and Cheesy Garlic Bread Loaf (page 55).

BEEF and BROCCOLI

Craving takeout? Skip it and make an amazing 30-minute takeout meal at home. This beef and broccoli has the best sauce, is loaded with fresh broccoli, and is easy to make on busy nights.

SERVES 4

PREP TIME: 15 MINS
COOK TIME: 15 MINS
TOTAL TIME: 30 MINS

INGREDIENTS

STIR-FRY SAUCE
- ½ cup hot water
- 6 Tablespoons low-sodium soy sauce
- 2 Tablespoons sesame oil
- 3 Tablespoons packed light brown sugar
- 1 Tablespoon minced garlic
- 1 teaspoon loosely packed grated fresh ginger
- 1½ Tablespoons cornstarch
- ½ teaspoon ground black pepper

STIR-FRY
- 2 Tablespoons olive oil or vegetable oil, divided
- 6 cups broccoli florets (about 1 pound)
- 1 pound flank steak, sliced very thin (see Julie's Notes) and cut into bite-size pieces
- 2 teaspoons sesame seeds for garnish, optional

INSTRUCTIONS

1. In a small bowl, combine all the sauce ingredients and whisk until the sugar is dissolved and the cornstarch is fully incorporated. Set aside.

2. For the stir-fry: Heat 1 Tablespoon of the oil in a large skillet over medium heat. Add the broccoli florets and sauté for 4 to 5 minutes, stirring and tossing several times, until the broccoli is bright green and crisp tender. Remove the broccoli from the pan and set aside.

3. Increase the heat to high and add the remaining 1 Tablespoon oil to the pan. Add the beef in a single layer and sauté 2 minutes per side, or until it is just cooked through.

4. Add the sauce to the skillet, reduce the heat to low, and simmer 3 to 4 minutes, until the sauce is thickened. Add the reserved broccoli and toss to combine. Garnish with the sesame seeds, if desired, and serve.

JULIE'S Notes

Cold steak is easier to slice thin, so start by placing the steak in the freezer for 30 minutes.

Serve with cooked white rice.

Scan for more tips!

DINNERS 177

SERVES 12

PREP TIME: 30 MINS

COOK TIME: 1 HR 30 MINS

TOTAL TIME: 2 HRS

LASAGNA

This is my mom's recipe, so you know it's delicious. Plus, it's quick and easy, with amazing flavor. The lasagna is full of ground beef, onion, spices, cottage cheese, and mozzarella cheese.

INGREDIENTS

- Nonstick cooking spray
- 2 pounds lean ground beef
- 1 yellow onion, minced
- 2 cloves garlic, minced
- 3 Tablespoons dried parsley, divided
- ½ teaspoon garlic salt
- ½ teaspoon dried oregano
- 4 (8-ounce) cans tomato sauce
- 1 (24-ounce) container cottage cheese
- 2 eggs, lightly beaten
- 1 teaspoon salt
- ½ cup grated parmesan cheese
- 6 lasagna noodles, cooked
- 1 pound mozzarella cheese, shredded

INSTRUCTIONS

1. Preheat the oven to 350 degrees Fahrenheit. Spray a 9-x-13-inch pan with nonstick cooking spray.

2. In a large frying pan, brown the hamburger, onion, and garlic over medium heat. Drain off any excess grease.

3. Add 1 Tablespoon of the parsley, the garlic salt, oregano, and tomato sauce. Bring to a boil over medium heat, then simmer over low heat for 30 minutes.

4. Meanwhile, in a large bowl, combine the cottage cheese, eggs, salt, the remaining 2 Tablespoons parsley, and the parmesan cheese.

5. Spread ½ cup of the meat sauce in the bottom of the pan. Arrange three lasagna noodles side by side on top so they don't overlap. Top with half the remaining meat sauce, half the cottage cheese mixture, then half the mozzarella cheese. Repeat with a layer of noodles, meat sauce, and cottage cheese.

6. Bake for 45 minutes. Top with the remaining mozzarella cheese and bake for 10 more minutes, or until the cheese is melted.

7. Let the lasagna stand for 10 to 15 minutes before serving.

JULIE'S Notes

Serve with Tossed Salad with Italian Dressing (page 64) and Cheesy Garlic Bread Loaf (page 55).

Scan for more tips!

178   JULIE'S EATS & TREATS COOKBOOK

GARLIC-BUTTER STEAK and POTATOES

This is a perfect dinner—tender, juicy pieces of steak with crispy potatoes tossed in garlic butter. Plus, it's ready in about 30 minutes.

SERVES 5

PREP TIME: 15 MINS
COOK TIME: 15 MINS
TOTAL TIME: 30 MINS

INGREDIENTS

- 1½ pounds sirloin steak, cut into 1-inch cubes
- 2 teaspoons beef dry rub (see Julie's Notes)
- 1 Tablespoon olive oil
- 4 Tablespoons salted butter, divided
- 1 pound Yukon gold potatoes, cut into ½-inch cubes (about 3½ cups)
- 1 teaspoon dried Italian seasoning
- 4 cloves garlic, minced
- Optional garnish: Chopped parsley

INSTRUCTIONS

1. Rub the steak cubes with the beef rub and set aside while you prepare the potatoes.

2. Heat a large cast-iron skillet or regular skillet over medium heat. Add the olive oil and 2 Tablespoons of the butter. When the butter has melted, add the potatoes and cook for 4 minutes without stirring. Sprinkle the Italian seasoning on the potatoes and stir. Continue cooking for 6 to 8 minutes, stirring a few times, until the potatoes are fork tender. Remove from the skillet and set aside.

3. Turn the heat to medium-high and add the remaining 2 Tablespoons butter to the skillet. When the butter has melted, add the seasoned steak and the garlic, making sure the steak is spread out in an even layer. Sear for 1 minute. Flip the steak pieces with a spatula or a fork and cook for 2 to 3 minutes more, until the steak is golden brown and cooked to your desired doneness.

4. Return the potatoes to the pan and toss to coat. Garnish with the chopped parsley, if desired, and serve immediately.

JULIE'S Notes

Pick whatever beef dry rub you like best. Or you can simply season to taste with salt and pepper.

Cut the steak and potatoes into the same size pieces so they cook evenly.

Serve with Oven-Roasted Vegetables (page 91).

Scan for more tips!

DINNERS

SERVES 4

PREP TIME: 10 MINS

COOK TIME: 30 MINS

TOTAL TIME: 40 MINS

SHEET PAN STEAK, POTATOES, *and* ASPARAGUS

Tender steak with crispy oven-roasted potatoes and asparagus are all baked on one baking sheet for an easy dinner.

INGREDIENTS

1½ pounds baby potatoes, halved

1 Tablespoon + 2 teaspoons olive oil

3 cloves garlic, minced, divided

1 teaspoon steak rub, divided

½ cup grated parmesan cheese, divided

1½ pounds rib eye steak

1 pound fresh asparagus, trimmed

INSTRUCTIONS

1. Preheat the oven to 375 degrees Fahrenheit. Position a baking rack in the middle of the oven.

2. Place the potatoes on a large baking sheet and toss with the 1 Tablespoon olive oil, one-third of the minced garlic, and ½ teaspoon of the steak rub. Bake the potatoes for 15 to 20 minutes, until they're tender and lightly browned.

3. While the potatoes are baking, in a small bowl combine the remaining minced garlic, remaining ½ teaspoon steak rub, 1 teaspoon of the oil, and ¼ cup of the parmesan cheese. Pat the steak dry and rub the seasoning over both sides.

4. Remove the potatoes from the oven and turn the broiler on high. Move the potatoes to one side of the baking sheet. Place the asparagus on the other side of the baking sheet and toss with the last 1 teaspoon oil, leaving enough room down the middle for the steak. Place the steak on the baking sheet between the potatoes and the asparagus. Lay a piece of aluminum foil over the potatoes to prevent them from burning when you broil the steak.

5. Return the pan to the oven and broil for 8 to 10 minutes, flipping the steak halfway through the cooking time, or until the steak is cooked to your liking.

6. Sprinkle the remaining ¼ cup parmesan cheese over the potatoes and serve.

Slow Cooker
FRENCH DIP SANDWICHES

SERVES 8

PREP TIME: 15 MINS
COOK TIME: 8 HRS 15 MINS
TOTAL TIME: 8 HRS 30 MINS

Roast beef is simmered all day in your slow cooker so it's falling-apart tender when you pile it high on your toasted hoagie roll and then melt provolone on the top. Don't forget to dunk it in the salty au jus to finish it off.

INGREDIENTS

- 1 (3- to 4-pound) chuck roast or bottom round beef roast, room temperature (see Julie's Notes)
- ½ teaspoon onion powder
- ½ teaspoon salt
- ¼ teaspoon ground black pepper
- 1 Tablespoon olive oil
- 1 (1.25-ounce) package dry au jus mix
- 1 (12-ounce) can beer
- 8 hoagie rolls
- 3 Tablespoons salted butter, melted
- ¼ teaspoon garlic powder
- 8 slices provolone cheese
- Optional garnish: Chopped parsley

INSTRUCTIONS

1. Season the roast with the onion powder, salt, and pepper. Heat the olive oil in a large skillet over medium heat and sear the roast on all sides.
2. Place the roast in a 6-quart slow cooker. Sprinkle the au jus mix over the roast, then pour in the beer. Cover the pot and cook on low for 8 hours. Transfer the meat to a serving plate and shred with two forks.
3. Set the oven to broil. Cut open the hoagie rolls and place them on a baking sheet, cut side up. In a small bowl, combine the melted butter and garlic powder, then brush over the rolls. Broil under low heat for 3 to 4 minutes, until the rolls are just turning golden brown.
4. Pile the cooked meat in the rolls and top with slices of cheese. Return to the broiler and broil just until the cheese has started to melt. Top the sandwiches with the parsley, if using.
5. Strain the liquid left in the slow cooker through a fine-mesh strainer. Serve the strained au jus with the sandwiches for dipping.

JULIE'S Notes

Let the roast rest at room temperature for at least 15 minutes before searing.

Serve with Oven-Roasted Vegetables (page 91).

Scan for more tips!

DINNERS 185

SERVES 6

PREP TIME: 10 MINS

COOK TIME: 4 OR 8 HRS

TOTAL TIME: 4 HRS 10 MINS OR 8 HRS 10 MINS

Slow Cooker MISSISSIPPI POT ROAST

Chuck roast becomes tender when it's cooked in the slow cooker with seasonings, beef broth, and pepperoncini—a mild Italian green pepper. It's an easy meal that's ready when you get home.

INGREDIENTS

- 1 (3- to 4-pound) chuck roast
- 1 (1-ounce) package ranch seasoning
- 2 cloves garlic, minced
- 1 (2.2-ounce) package French onion soup mix
- 3 cups beef broth
- 6 pepperoncini plus ½ cup juice from the jar

INSTRUCTIONS

1. Place the chuck roast in a 6-quart slow cooker and sprinkle with the ranch seasoning, garlic, and French onion soup mix. Pour the beef broth and pepperoncini juice into the slow cooker. Add the pepperoncini and cover the pot.
2. Cook on low for 8 hours, or on high for 4 hours.
3. When the roast is done, remove 1 cup of juice from the slow cooker and set it aside (see Julie's Notes). Use two big forks to shred the rest of the roast right in the pot.

JULIE'S *Notes*

Serve over mashed potatoes, noodles, or rice, using the reserved juice as gravy.

Serve with Oven-Roasted Vegetables (page 91).

Scan for more tips!

186 JULIE'S EATS & TREATS COOKBOOK

Stuffed ZUCCHINI BOATS

SERVES 4

PREP TIME: 10 MINS
COOK TIME: 35 MINS
TOTAL TIME: 45 MINS

This is an easy, low-carb dinner that's delicious and healthy. Hollowed out zucchini halves are filled with a hearty ground sausage mixture, then topped with cheese and baked until nicely browned.

INGREDIENTS

- 4 medium zucchini
- 2 teaspoons olive oil
- 1 pound ground mild Italian sausage
- ½ cup finely diced yellow onion
- 2 teaspoons minced garlic
- ½ teaspoon dried Italian seasoning
- 1½ cups marinara sauce
- ¾ cup shredded mozzarella cheese
- Optional garnish: Chopped parsley

INSTRUCTIONS

1. Preheat the oven to 400 degrees Fahrenheit. Line a large baking sheet with aluminum foil for easy cleanup.

2. Trim off the ends of the zucchini, then cut them in half lengthwise. Scoop the flesh out with a spoon and discard. Place the zucchini halves on the baking sheet.

3. Heat the olive oil in a large skillet over medium-high heat. Add the sausage and cook for 4 to 5 minutes, breaking up the meat with a spatula. Add the onion and cook for an additional 4 minutes, or until the onion is translucent and soft. Add the garlic and Italian seasoning and cook for 30 seconds, or until fragrant. Pour the marinara sauce into the pan and bring to a simmer.

4. Spoon the meat mixture into the zucchini shells and top with the shredded mozzarella cheese.

5. Bake for 20 to 25 minutes, until the zucchini is tender and the cheese is melted and golden brown. Sprinkle with the parsley and serve immediately.

JULIE'S Notes

Serve with Roasted Sweet Potatoes (page 84).

Scan for more tips!

DINNERS 189

SERVES 6

PREP TIME: 15 MINS
COOK TIME: 30 MINS
TOTAL TIME: 45 MINS

PIZZA *Sliders*

Here's a perfect, quick and easy dinner for any night of the week, or a great appetizer for a hungry gang. Slider buns are layered with pizza sauce, fresh mozzarella, and pepperoni, then brushed with a seasoned parmesan butter.

INGREDIENTS

Nonstick cooking spray
12 slider buns or Hawaiian rolls
¾ to 1 cup pizza sauce or marinara sauce
6 ounces pepperoni slices
8 ounces fresh mozzarella cheese

½ cup grated parmesan cheese
¼ cup salted butter, melted
½ teaspoon garlic powder
½ teaspoon dried basil
½ teaspoon dried oregano

INSTRUCTIONS

1. Preheat the oven to 350 degrees Fahrenheit. Lightly spray a 9-x-13-inch baking dish with nonstick cooking spray.

2. Cut the slider buns in half and set the tops aside. Place the bottom halves in the baking dish and spread with the sauce. Add the pepperoni slices to the buns, using as many as you like (I use the whole package). Slice the mozzarella into 12 slices and place a slice on each bun. Cover each slider with the top half of a bun.

3. In a small bowl, thoroughly combine the parmesan cheese, melted butter, garlic powder, basil, and oregano. Brush the seasoned butter over the tops of the buns.

4. Cover the pan with aluminum foil and bake for 20 to 25 minutes. Remove the foil and bake for an additional 5 minutes, until the tops of the buns are toasted. Serve immediately.

JULIE'S *Notes*

Serve with Tossed Salad with Italian Dressing (page 64).

Scan for more tips!

One-Pot PIZZA PASTA

Here's an easy one-pot meal that kids love and is ready in 30 minutes. With corkscrew pasta, cheese, and pepperoni, it has all the flavors of pizza in a pasta recipe.

PREP TIME: 15 MINS
COOK TIME: 10 MINS
TOTAL TIME: 25 MINS

SERVES 4

INGREDIENTS

- 8 ounces uncooked corkscrew pasta
- 2 cups low-sodium chicken broth
- 1 (14-ounce) can diced tomatoes with basil, garlic, and oregano
- ½ cup milk
- 1 teaspoon garlic powder
- ½ teaspoon dried oregano
- 2 cups shredded mozzarella cheese
- ½ cup mini pepperoni slices
- Grated parmesan cheese, for topping

INSTRUCTIONS

1. In a large pot, bring the pasta, broth, canned tomatoes, milk, garlic powder, and oregano to a boil. Cover and cook at a medium boil, stirring frequently, for about 10 minutes, or until the pasta is al dente. Most of the liquid should have evaporated. If it hasn't, remove the lid and let the pasta cook for an additional few minutes, or until the liquid has mostly evaporated.

2. Mix in the mozzarella cheese and pepperoni and stir until the cheese is melted and combined. Top with parmesan cheese and serve immediately.

JULIE'S Notes

Serve with Tossed Salad with Italian Dressing (page 64).

Scan for more tips!

DINNERS 193

SERVES 8

PREP TIME: 15 MINS
COOK TIME: 65 MINS
TOTAL TIME: 1 HR 20 MINS

HAM and POTATO CASSEROLE

Got leftover ham to use up? Make this hearty casserole that is cheesy, creamy, and delicious.

INGREDIENTS

- Nonstick cooking spray
- 1 (10.75-ounce) can condensed cream of mushroom soup
- 1 cup whole milk
- ½ cup sour cream
- ½ teaspoon garlic powder
- ½ teaspoon onion powder
- ½ teaspoon salt
- ½ teaspoon ground black pepper
- 2 pounds russet potatoes, peeled and diced small
- 2 cups cubed ham
- 2 cups shredded Colby jack cheese

INSTRUCTIONS

1. Preheat the oven to 400 degrees Fahrenheit. Spray a 9-x-13-inch baking dish with nonstick cooking spray.

2. In a large bowl, mix together the cream of mushroom soup, milk, sour cream, garlic powder, onion powder, salt, and pepper.

3. Evenly spread the diced potatoes on the bottom of the baking dish. Spread the ham evenly over the potatoes. Pour the soup mixture over the ham and potatoes.

4. Cover with aluminum foil and bake for 45 to 50 minutes, until the potatoes are cooked through.

5. Remove the foil and sprinkle the cheese on top. Bake, uncovered, for 10 to 15 minutes, until the cheese is melted and the edges are bubbling.

JULIE'S Notes

Serve with Oven-Roasted Vegetables (page 91).

Scan for more tips!

Parmesan-Crusted PORK CHOPS

These tender, juicy boneless pork chops have a crunchy coating. Try them if you are tired of chewy, dry pork.

SERVES 4

PREP TIME: 15 MINS
COOK TIME: 15 MINS
TOTAL TIME: 30 MINS

INGREDIENTS

- ¼ cup grated parmesan cheese
- 2 Tablespoons Italian-style bread crumbs
- 1 teaspoon dried parsley
- ½ teaspoon garlic powder
- ¼ teaspoon smoked paprika
- ¼ teaspoon ground black pepper
- 4 boneless pork chops
- 2 Tablespoons olive oil

INSTRUCTIONS

1. Preheat the oven to 450 degrees Fahrenheit.

2. Mix the parmesan cheese, breadcrumbs, parsley, garlic powder, paprika, and pepper together in a pie plate. Dip each pork chop in the breadcrumb mixture, patting to make the crumbs stick if needed.

3. Heat the olive oil in a large frying pan over medium-high heat. Swirl the pan to coat it with oil. Add the coated pork chops and sauté for 2 minutes on each side, until golden brown. Place in a glass baking dish (or leave them in the pan if it is oven safe).

4. Bake the chops in the oven for 8 to 10 minutes, until the internal temperature reaches 145 degrees Fahrenheit. Let rest for 5 minutes before serving.

JULIE'S Notes

Serve with Bacon-Wrapped Green Beans (page 92) and Cheesy Garlic-Butter Pasta (page 83).

Scan for more tips!

DINNERS 197

SERVES 4

PREP TIME: 10 MINS
COOK TIME: 20 MINS
TOTAL TIME: 30 MINS

Parmesan-Crusted TILAPIA

This easy fish dish has a simple panko-parmesan coating that gives it a tasty and crunchy crust—and it's ready in just 30 minutes.

INGREDIENTS

- Nonstick cooking spray
- ½ cup panko breadcrumbs
- ½ cup grated parmesan cheese
- 3 Tablespoons salted butter, melted
- 4 tilapia fillets
- Optional garnish: Chopped parsley

INSTRUCTIONS

1. Preheat the oven to 425 degrees Fahrenheit. Spray a large baking sheet with nonstick cooking spray.

2. In a medium bowl, mix the panko crumbs, parmesan cheese, and melted butter.

3. Pat the tilapia fillets dry with paper towels, then lay the fillets on the baking sheet. Top with the panko crumb mixture. Bake for 15 to 20 minutes, until the tilapia flakes easily with a fork in the thickest part.

JULIE'S Notes

Serve with Bacon-Wrapped Green Beans (page 92) and Cheesy Garlic-Butter Pasta (page 83).

Scan for more tips!

SHRIMP *Boil*

SERVES 6

PREP TIME: 10 MINS
COOK TIME: 18 MINS
TOTAL TIME: 28 MINS

A mixture of corn on the cob pieces, shrimp, smoked sausage, and baby potatoes is cooked in a seasoned broth, then tossed in seasoned butter. And that's not even the best part! The best part is that it's ready in about 30 minutes.

INGREDIENTS

- 4 lemons
- 1 medium yellow onion, cut into large pieces
- 4 cloves garlic, smashed
- ⅓ cup seafood seasoning, such as Old Bay
- 1 pound small red potatoes, each cut in half
- 4 ears corn, each cut into 4 pieces
- 1 pound smoked sausage, kielbasa, or andouille, cut into 1-inch pieces
- 2 pounds jumbo shrimp, peeled and deveined, tails on
- ½ cup unsalted butter
- 2 Tablespoons chopped fresh parsley, plus more for garnish
- ½ teaspoon salt
- ½ teaspoon ground black pepper

INSTRUCTIONS

1. Fill a large pot with water. Quarter two lemons and add them to the water. Add the onion, garlic, and seafood seasoning. Bring the water to a boil over high heat.
2. Add the potatoes to the boiling water and cook for 10 to 12 minutes, until they're just barely fork tender.
3. Add the corn and sausage and cook for 5 to 6 minutes.
4. Add the shrimp and cook for 2 to 3 minutes, until they turn pink.
5. Drain the potatoes, corn, sausage, and shrimp in a colander and transfer everything to a large baking sheet.
6. In a microwave-safe bowl, melt the butter in the microwave. Add the parsley, salt, and pepper and whisk to combine. Pour half the butter mixture over the shrimp mixture and stir to coat. Reserve the remaining butter mixture for serving.
7. Cut the remaining 2 lemons into wedges. Garnish the shrimp mixture with the lemon wedges and chopped parsley. Sprinkle on some additional seafood seasoning to taste, if desired. Serve immediately with the reserved butter mixture for dipping.

Scan for more tips!

DINNERS 201

SERVES 6

PREP TIME: 15 MINS
COOK TIME: 10 MINS
TOTAL TIME: 25 MINS

SHRIMP *Pasta*

You get so much flavor from the grilled shrimp and roasted cherry tomatoes, and it's all topped with parmesan cheese. It's ready in under 30 minutes, yet tastes like it came from a restaurant.

INGREDIENTS

- 8 ounces uncooked linguine pasta
- 16 cherry tomatoes
- 2 Tablespoons olive oil, divided
- 1 pound uncooked large shrimp, peeled and deveined, tails on
- ½ teaspoon ground black pepper
- ¼ teaspoon salt
- ¼ teaspoon garlic powder
- 2 Tablespoons salted butter
- ¼ cup grated parmesan cheese
- 2 Tablespoons chopped fresh basil

INSTRUCTIONS

1. Prepare a grill for medium heat.
2. Cook the linguine in a large pot of salted boiling water until al dente, according to the package directions.
3. Meanwhile, thread the tomatoes onto skewers and brush with about half of the olive oil. Thread the shrimp onto their own skewers and brush with the remaining olive oil. In a small bowl, mix the pepper, salt, and garlic powder. Sprinkle the seasoning over the shrimp.
4. Grill the shrimp and tomatoes, covered, over medium heat for 3 to 4 minutes on each side, until the shrimp turn pink and the tomatoes are slightly softened.
5. Drain the linguine, reserving ¼ cup of the pasta water.
6. In the same pasta pot, melt the butter over medium heat. Add the linguine and reserved pasta water and toss to combine. Remove the shrimp and tomatoes from the skewers, and toss with the pasta. Sprinkle the parmesan cheese and basil on top of the pasta and serve.

JULIE'S *Notes*

Make sure to soak wooden skewers in water a minimum of 30 minutes to prevent them from burning on the grill.

If you prefer not to grill your shrimp and tomatoes, you can cook them on the stovetop in a cast-iron grill pan over medium heat, or simply throw them in a skillet and sauté them.

Serve with Tossed Salad with Italian Dressing (page 64).

Scan for more tips!

Monster Cookie Bars, page 241

Desserts

Hot Fudge Sauce // 206

Oreo Ice Cream Dessert // 209

Buster Bar Dessert // 210

The Best Rice Krispie Treats // 213

No-Bake Cheesecake // 214

Lemon Bundt Cake // 217

Strawberry Poke Cake // 218

Oreo Poke Cake // 221

Strawberry Crisp // 222

Apple Crisp // 225

Strawberry Pie // 226

Fruit Pizza // 229

Banana Bars // 230

Pumpkin Bars // 233

Peanut Butter Cereal Bars // 234

Salted Nut Roll Bars // 237

Knock You Naked Bars // 238

Monster Cookie Bars // 241

Oatmeal Cookies // 242

Chocolate Chip Cookies // 245

Pumpkin Snickerdoodle Cookies // 246

Reese's Pieces Peanut Butter Cookies // 249

Chocolate Cherry Brownies // 250

1 CUP, SERVING 12

PREP TIME: 5 MINS

COOK TIME: 5 MINS

TOTAL TIME: 10 MINS

HOT FUDGE *Sauce*

We used to beg my mom to make this when we were kids: a delicious smooth and rich chocolate sauce with only five ingredients. It's the perfect topping for a big bowl of ice cream.

INGREDIENTS

- 1 cup white granulated sugar
- 2 Tablespoons unsweetened cocoa powder
- ½ cup cream
- 1 teaspoon salted butter
- 1 teaspoon vanilla extract

INSTRUCTIONS

1. In a small saucepan, mix the sugar and cocoa until combined. Add the cream and stir.
2. Bring to a boil over medium heat and boil for 1 minute.
3. Remove from the heat and add the butter and vanilla. Stir until the butter is melted. Serve immediately.

JULIE'S *Notes*

To store leftovers, let sauce completely cool and store in an airtight container. Refrigerate for up to a week.

To reheat, warm in a saucepan over low heat. Or you can microwave the sauce in a microwave-safe container in 20- to 30-second increments, stirring in between each.

Scan for more tips!

206   JULIE'S EATS & TREATS COOKBOOK

OREO ICE CREAM *Dessert*

A delicious Oreo crust topped with vanilla ice cream, hot fudge, and whipped topping makes this easy five-ingredient dessert the perfect no-bake treat for summer.

SERVES 6

PREP TIME: 15 MINS

CHILL TIME: 4 HRS 30 MINS

TOTAL TIME: 4 HRS 45 MINS

INGREDIENTS

1 (19.1-ounce) package Oreo cookies, divided

⅓ cup salted butter, melted

½ gallon vanilla ice cream, softened

2 (8-ounce) tubs Cool Whip, thawed, divided

1 (16-ounce) jar hot fudge sauce

INSTRUCTIONS

1. Place the Oreos in a gallon-size resealable bag. Using a rolling pin, crush the cookies into medium-size chunks. Measure out 1½ cups and set aside. Leave the rest in the bag.

2. Add the melted butter to the bag and shake to combine. Pour the Oreo mixture into a 9-x-13-inch baking dish, spreading it out evenly.

3. In a large bowl, combine the softened ice cream, ¾ cup of the reserved crushed Oreos, and 1 container of the whipped topping. Gently stir to combine.

4. Spread the ice cream mixture in an even layer on top of the crushed Oreos in the baking dish. Cover the dish and freeze until the ice cream is set, about 2 hours.

5. Remove the lid from the fudge sauce jar and warm the fudge in the microwave for about 45 seconds, until it's spreadable. Carefully drizzle it over the ice cream and spread evenly with a spatula. Do not warm the fudge too much or it will melt into the ice cream. Cover the dish, put back in the freezer, and freeze until set, about 30 minutes.

6. Evenly spread the remaining tub of whipped topping over the fudge. Then top with the remaining crushed Oreos. Cover and freeze for 2 hours, or until firm.

JULIE'S *Notes*

You can store this in the freezer for up to a week.

Remove the dessert from the freezer 10 minutes before serving, so it's easier to cut. Then dip a knife into hot water to make slicing easier, and wipe the blade clean periodically while cutting.

SERVES 20

PREP TIME: 15 MINS
COOK TIME: 10 MINS
CHILL TIME: 4 HRS
TOTAL TIME: 4 HRS 25 MINS

BUSTER BAR *Dessert*

The perfect ice cream dessert for summer has an Oreo crust, a layer of vanilla ice cream, and a topping of homemade fudge and peanuts.

INGREDIENTS

Nonstick cooking spray

1 (14.3-ounce) package Oreo cookies, crushed

½ cup salted butter, melted

½ gallon vanilla ice cream, softened

1 cup (6 ounces) chocolate chips

1 (12-ounce) can evaporated milk

½ cup salted butter

2 cups powdered sugar

1 cup dry-roasted peanuts

INSTRUCTIONS

1. Lightly spray a 9-x-13-inch baking pan with nonstick cooking spray.

2. In a large bowl, mix together the crushed Oreos and the melted butter. Pat the Oreo mixture into the bottom of the prepared pan. Place the pan in the freezer for at least 15 minutes.

3. Spread the softened ice cream evenly across the Oreo crust. Place the pan back in the freezer while you prepare the fudge sauce.

4. In a small saucepan, combine the chocolate chips, evaporated milk, butter, and the powdered sugar. Stir together and bring to a boil over medium-high heat. Boil for 8 minutes, stirring constantly. Remove from the heat and cool until it's completely cold. (Do *not* pour warm sauce over the ice cream!)

5. Once the fudge has cooled, spread it evenly over the top of the ice cream. Then sprinkle the peanuts over the top of the fudge sauce. Cover and freeze for at least 4 hours or overnight.

JULIE'S *Notes*

When you're ready to serve, let set at room temperature for 5 to 10 minutes, then cut into bars.

Store in the freezer for up to a week.

Scan for more tips!

The Best RICE KRISPIE TREATS

20 TREATS

PREP TIME: 10 MINS
COOL TIME: 1 HR
TOTAL TIME: 1 HR 10 MINS

Think ooey, gooey, and loaded with marshmallows. These are thick, chewy, and always disappear quickly.

INGREDIENTS

- Nonstick cooking spray
- 2 (10-ounce) bags mini marshmallows, divided
- ¾ cup salted butter, sliced into thin slabs
- 1 teaspoon vanilla extract
- 8½ cups Rice Krispies cereal

INSTRUCTIONS

1. Spray a 9-x-13-inch baking pan with nonstick cooking spray or line with heavy duty aluminum foil greased with nonstick cooking spray. (If you're using foil, drape it over the sides of the pan so it overhangs for easy removal of the bars.)

2. Measure out 2 cups marshmallows and set aside. Place the butter and the remaining marshmallows in a large microwave-safe bowl. Microwave for 2 minutes. Remove and stir until the butter and marshmallows are melted and combined. Add the vanilla and stir until combined.

3. Quickly mix in the Rice Krispies and stir until they are completely coated with the marshmallows. Add the reserved marshmallows and stir until they are softened and partially melted. (You do not want them to completely melt, as they provide those delicious pockets of marshmallow goo.)

4. Press the mixture into the prepared pan. You can butter or moisten your fingers with water to help press the mixture into the pan without getting it stuck to your fingers, or use the butter wrapper to push the mixture into the pan. Let cool at room temperature for at least 1 hour.

5. If you used foil, use it to lift the treats onto a cutting board and cut into pieces. Otherwise cut them in the pan.

JULIE'S Notes

If you do not want to microwave the butter and marshmallows, you can simply heat them in a saucepan over medium heat, stirring frequently, until completely melted.

Store the treats in an airtight container at room temperature for up to 2 days, or refrigerate for up to 5 days.

Scan for more tips!

DESSERTS 213

SERVES 8

PREP TIME: 20 MINS
COOK TIME: 10 MINS
CHILL TIME: 4 HRS
TOTAL TIME: 4 HRS 30 MINS

No-Bake CHEESECAKE

This smooth, creamy cheesecake with a delicious graham cracker crust sets up perfectly in the refrigerator. It's light, sweet, and refreshing.

INGREDIENTS

GRAHAM CRACKER CRUST

1½ cups crushed graham cracker crumbs (12 to 14 sheets)
½ cup salted butter, melted
¼ cup packed brown sugar

TOPPING

1 (21-ounce) can cherry pie filling

CHEESECAKE FILLING

2 (8-ounce) packages cream cheese, room temperature
¼ cup sour cream
1 cup powdered sugar
1 teaspoon vanilla extract
1 cup heavy cream, cold
1 teaspoon cornstarch

INSTRUCTIONS

1. Preheat the oven to 350 degrees Fahrenheit.

2. In a medium bowl, combine the graham cracker crumbs, melted butter, and brown sugar with a fork until well combined. Press the graham cracker mixture into the bottom and 1½ inches up the sides of a 9-inch pie plate. Bake for 10 minutes. Remove from the oven and let cool.

3. To make the filling, in a large bowl, beat the cream cheese and sour cream with an electric mixer until smooth. Add the powdered sugar and vanilla and beat until combined.

4. In a medium bowl, beat the cream on low for 1 minute. Add the cornstarch, turn the mixer to high, and beat for an additional 3 to 4 minutes, until stiff peaks form. Gently fold the whipped cream into the cream cheese mixture.

5. Spread the cheesecake filling into the cooled pie crust, cover with plastic wrap, and refrigerate 4 hours or overnight, until it is firm.

6. Top with canned cherry pie filling or your favorite toppings and serve.

JULIE'S Notes

You can use a premade graham cracker crust for this recipe instead of making one.

If you're not in the mood for cherry topping, you can top the cheesecake with other delicious things, such as strawberry or blueberry sauce, caramel or chocolate syrup, fresh fruit, or whatever you like.

Cover the cheesecake and refrigerate for up to 5 days.

Scan for more tips!

LEMON BUNDT *Cake*

Here's a delicious lemon cake baked in a Bundt pan. With a lemon icing, it is not only pretty but also tender, moist, and so flavorful.

SERVES 12

PREP TIME: 20 MINS
COOK TIME: 55 MINS
TOTAL TIME: 1 HR 15 MINS

INGREDIENTS

CAKE
- Nonstick cooking spray
- Flour for pan
- 1 (15.25-ounce) box lemon cake mix
- 1 (3.4-ounce) package lemon instant pudding mix
- 1 cup water
- ½ cup vegetable oil
- 4 eggs

ICING
- 1 cup powdered sugar
- 1 Tablespoon + 1 teaspoon lemon juice
- 1 teaspoon vegetable oil

INSTRUCTIONS

1. Preheat the oven to 350 degrees Fahrenheit. Grease and flour a 10- to 12-cup Bundt pan.
2. Combine all the cake ingredients in a large bowl and beat with an electric mixer for 2 minutes.
3. Pour into the Bundt pan. Bake for 45 to 55 minutes, until a cake tester inserted in the center comes out clean. Cool in the pan for 25 minutes, then invert onto a cake rack. Cool completely.
4. In a medium bowl, thoroughly combine all the icing ingredients. Drizzle the icing over the cooled cake.

JULIE'S *Notes*

Store leftovers in an airtight container at room temperature for 2 to 3 days or in the refrigerator for up to 5 days. You can also freeze leftovers for up to 3 months, but first wrap individual pieces in plastic wrap or aluminum foil and place in a freezer bag.

Scan for more tips!

DESSERTS 217

SERVES 16

PREP TIME: 15 MINS

COOK TIME: 30 MINS

CHILL TIME: 6 HRS

TOTAL TIME: 6 HRS 45 MINS

STRAWBERRY POKE *Cake*

This cake starts with a box mix and is topped with strawberry Jell-O, vanilla pudding, and Cool Whip. Poke cake is the perfect comfort food dessert. And this quick and easy recipe is also great for entertaining.

INGREDIENTS

- 1 (16.25-ounce) package white cake mix + ingredients to prepare
- 1 (0.3-ounce) box Jell-O sugar-free strawberry gelatin mix
- 1½ cups water, divided
- 1 (1-ounce) box sugar-free vanilla instant pudding mix
- 2 cups milk
- 1 (8-ounce) container Cool Whip, thawed

INSTRUCTIONS

1. Bake the cake according to the package instructions in a 9-x-13-inch pan, using the ingredients required. While the cake is still hot, immediately poke holes in the top with the handle of a wooden spoon, going about halfway into the cake. Cover and refrigerate for 3 to 4 hours.

2. Make the Jell-O according to package instructions with 1 cup boiling water and ½ cup cold water. Mix them all together in a large measuring cup until the gelatin is dissolved. Pour over the chilled cake. This will seem like a lot of liquid, but the cake will absorb it and it won't become mush.

3. Return the cake to the fridge while you prepare the pudding. In a medium bowl, mix the pudding mix with the milk. Let it sit until the pudding is soft set with a spoonable consistency, about 5 minutes.

4. Spread the pudding over the top of the cake and top with the Cool Whip. Refrigerate for at least 2 hours or overnight to set.

JULIE'S *Notes*

Store, covered, in the refrigerator for up to 3 days.

Scan for more tips!

218   JULIE'S EATS & TREATS COOKBOOK

OREO POKE *Cake*

My husband, Jason, loves this cake and requests it for his birthday every year. It's chocolate cake topped with Oreo pudding, Cool Whip, and crushed Oreos.

SERVES 20

PREP TIME: 15 MINS
COOK TIME: 30 MINS
CHILL TIME: 1 HR
TOTAL TIME: 1 HR 45 MINS

INGREDIENTS

- 1 (15.25-ounce) box chocolate cake mix + ingredients to prepare
- 2 (4.2-ounce) packages Jell-O Oreo instant pudding mix
- 4 cups 2% milk
- 1 (8-ounce) container Cool Whip, thawed
- 1 cup crushed Oreo cookies

INSTRUCTIONS

1. Bake the cake according to package instructions in a 9-x-13-inch pan, using the ingredients required. While the cake is still hot, poke holes in the top with the handle of a wooden spoon, going about halfway into the cake. Let the cake cool while you prepare the pudding.

2. In a medium bowl, whisk together the pudding mix and milk. Make sure to whisk out all of the lumps. Let the pudding mixture sit for about 2 minutes. You want it somewhat thickened but not set like pudding.

3. Pour the pudding mixture over the warm cake. Allow the cake to cool for a few minutes. Then put it in the fridge to set up, which takes about 1 hour.

4. When the cake is set, spread Cool Whip over the top and sprinkle with crushed Oreo cookies (see Julie's Notes).

JULIE'S *Notes*

If you don't plan on enjoying all the cake at once, just sprinkle Oreos on the part you will serve as the cookies will get soggy if they sit too long on the topping.

Store, covered, in the refrigerator for up to 3 days.

Scan for more tips!

DESSERTS 221

SERVES 6

PREP TIME: 15 MINS
COOK TIME: 40 MINS
TOTAL TIME: 55 MINS

STRAWBERRY *Crisp*

This quick and easy crisp is full of juicy strawberries and topped with a buttery brown sugar–oat crumble. Serve it warm with vanilla ice cream.

INGREDIENTS

FILLING
- Nonstick cooking spray
- 5 cups halved or quartered fresh strawberries
- 2 Tablespoons orange juice
- ¼ cup white granulated sugar
- ¼ cup all-purpose flour

TOPPING
- ⅔ cup old-fashioned rolled oats
- ⅔ cup all-purpose flour
- ⅓ cup white granulated sugar
- ¼ cup packed light brown sugar
- ¼ teaspoon salt
- ¼ teaspoon ground cinnamon
- ½ cup unsalted butter, melted

INSTRUCTIONS

1. Preheat the oven to 350 degrees Fahrenheit. Spray a 9½-inch deep-dish pie plate or a similar baking dish with nonstick cooking spray.

2. In a large bowl, combine all the filling ingredients. Stir gently until well combined. Dump into the baking dish.

3. In a separate large bowl, combine the oats, flour, white and brown sugars, salt, and cinnamon. Add the melted butter and stir until well combined. Sprinkle the topping over the filling, pressing some of it together with your fingers to form clumps.

4. Bake for 30 to 40 minutes, until the fruit is bubbling and juicy and the topping is light golden brown. Cool slightly before serving.

Scan for more tips!

APPLE *Crisp*

SERVES 8

PREP TIME: 20 MINS
COOK TIME: 45 MINS
TOTAL TIME: 1 HR 5 MINS

This quick and easy crisp recipe is full of juicy apples, cinnamon, and sugar—and the best part of all is the amazing oatmeal streusel on top. A scoop of this topped with vanilla ice cream and a drizzle of caramel is the ultimate fall dessert. And it's so easy!

INGREDIENTS

Nonstick cooking spray

TOPPING
- 1 cup salted butter, melted
- 1 cup packed brown sugar
- 1 cup all-purpose flour
- 1 cup old-fashioned rolled oats
- 1 teaspoon baking powder

FILLING
- 8 cups peeled, cored, and thinly sliced Granny Smith apples (8 to 10 apples)
- ¾ cup packed brown sugar
- 1 Tablespoon ground cinnamon
- 1 Tablespoon cornstarch

INSTRUCTIONS

1. Preheat the oven to 350 degrees Fahrenheit. Lightly spray a 9-x-13-inch baking dish with nonstick cooking spray.

2. To make the topping, in a medium bowl mix all the ingredients. Refrigerate while you prepare the filling.

3. Place the apple slices in a large bowl and toss with the sugar, cinnamon, and cornstarch to combine. Dump the apple mixture into the baking dish and spread in an even layer. Top with the oat crumble mixture, occasionally pressing some of it together with your hands to form clumps.

4. Bake for 40 to 45 minutes, until the topping is golden brown, the apples are tender, and juices are bubbling around the edges of the pan. Cool slightly and serve warm.

Scan for more tips!

DESSERTS

SERVES 8

PREP TIME: 10 MINS

COOK TIME: 20 MINS

CHILL TIME: 2 HRS

TOTAL TIME: 2 HRS 30 MINS

STRAWBERRY *Pie*

With only five ingredients (plus water), this quick and easy pie is the perfect summertime dessert. It's made with a frozen pie crust, strawberry Jell-O, and fresh strawberries. Top it off with homemade whipped cream or Cool Whip.

INGREDIENTS

- 1 (9-inch) frozen pie crust
- 4 cups fresh strawberries, sliced
- 1½ cups water
- ¾ cup white granulated sugar
- 2 Tablespoons cornstarch
- 1 (3-ounce) package Jell-O strawberry gelatin mix

INSTRUCTIONS

1. Bake the pie crust according to the package directions. Cool.
2. Place the strawberries in the cooled pie crust.
3. Combine the water, sugar, and cornstarch in a small saucepan. Bring to a boil over medium-high heat and cook for 2 minutes. Add the Jell-O mix and stir until dissolved. Slowly pour the Jell-O over the berries. Chill in the refrigerator until set, 2 to 4 hours.

JULIE'S *Notes*

Store, covered, in the refrigerator until you're ready to serve. If you have leftovers, cover and store in refrigerator for up to 4 days.

Scan for more tips!

Fruit PIZZA

A giant sugar cookie is topped with a cream cheese frosting and your favorite fruit. It's beautiful, delicious, and oh so good!

SERVES 8

PREP TIME: 25 MINS
COOK TIME: 15 MINS
TOTAL TIME: 40 MINS

INGREDIENTS

SUGAR COOKIE CRUST
- Nonstick cooking spray
- 1 cup unsalted butter, softened
- 1 cup white granulated sugar
- 1 teaspoon vanilla extract
- 1 egg
- 2¾ cups all-purpose flour
- 2 teaspoons baking powder
- ½ teaspoon salt

CREAM CHEESE TOPPING
- 8 ounces cream cheese, softened
- ¼ cup unsalted butter, softened
- 2 cups powdered sugar
- ½ teaspoon vanilla extract

FRUIT
- ½ cup diced strawberries
- ½ cup blueberries
- ½ cup blackberries
- ½ cup raspberries
- ¼ cup chopped kiwis (1 or 2)
- ½ (15-ounce) can mandarin oranges, drained

INSTRUCTIONS

1. Preheat the oven to 350 degrees Fahrenheit. Lightly grease a 12-inch pizza pan with nonstick cooking spray.

2. Make the sugar cookie crust: In a large bowl, cream the butter and sugar with an electric hand mixer or stand mixer until light and fluffy, about 2 minutes. Add the vanilla and egg and mix for another 30 seconds or so. Add the flour, baking powder, and salt and mix just until combined.

3. Press the dough in an even layer on the pizza pan. Bake for 14 to 16 minutes, until the crust is lightly browned. Cool the crust completely before moving on to the next step.

4. To make the topping, beat the cream cheese and butter with an electric hand mixer or stand mixer until smooth, about 2 minutes. Add the powdered sugar and vanilla and beat until fully combined.

5. Spread in an even layer over the cooled crust. Decorate the top with the fruit. Cover with plastic wrap and refrigerate for up to a day until you're ready to cut and serve your pizza.

JULIE'S Notes

Yes, I've tested this recipe with prepared cookie dough and it works well. I use dough that is already portioned into 24 cookie dough balls—just press them into the pan to make one unified crust and reduce the baking time to about 10 minutes. The crust won't be as thick as the homemade one, but it will work fine.

Scan for more tips!

DESSERTS 229

20 BARS

PREP TIME: 15 MINS
COOK TIME: 25 MINS
TOTAL TIME: 40 MINS

BANANA Bars

These bars are topped with cream cheese frosting and so soft and tender. This is a trusted family favorite—no-fail and always a hit.

INGREDIENTS

BARS
Nonstick cooking spray
½ cup salted butter, softened
2 cups white granulated sugar
3 eggs
3 medium ripe bananas, mashed
1 teaspoon vanilla extract
2 cups all-purpose flour
1 teaspoon baking soda
Pinch of salt

FROSTING
¼ cup salted butter, softened
4 ounces cream cheese, softened
2¼ cups powdered sugar
1 teaspoon vanilla extract

INSTRUCTIONS

1. Preheat the oven to 350 degrees Fahrenheit. Lightly spray a 10-x-15-inch baking dish with nonstick cooking spray.

2. To make the bars: In a large bowl with an electric hand mixer or stand mixer, cream the butter and sugar. Beat in the eggs, bananas, and vanilla.

3. In a medium bowl, combine the flour, baking soda, and salt. Add to the banana mixture and mix well.

4. Pour the batter into the prepared baking pan. Bake for 25 minutes, or until a toothpick inserted into center of the bars comes out clean. Cool in the pan or on a wire rack.

5. For the frosting, in a large bowl with an electric hand mixer or stand mixer, cream together the butter and cream cheese. Gradually add the powdered sugar and vanilla. Beat well. If you want it thicker, add a little more powdered sugar.

6. Spread the frosting over the cooled bars. Cover and store in the refrigerator until serving, or up to 3 days. When you're ready to serve, cut into bars.

Scan for more tips!

PUMPKIN *Bars*

20 BARS

PREP TIME: 15 MINS
COOK TIME: 25 MINS
TOTAL TIME: 40 MINS

These tender, moist, and delicious bars are rich and pumpkin-y, and topped with a cream cheese frosting that's spiced with cinnamon to make them mouthwatering. This is the ultimate fall dessert—perfect for when you need to bring a treat to an event.

INGREDIENTS

PUMPKIN BARS
- 4 eggs
- 1⅔ cups white granulated sugar
- 1 cup canola oil
- 1 (15-ounce) can plain pumpkin purée
- 2 cups all-purpose flour
- 2 teaspoons baking powder
- 1 teaspoon baking soda
- 2 teaspoons ground cinnamon
- 1 teaspoon salt

FROSTING
- 3 ounces cream cheese, softened
- ½ cup salted butter
- 1 teaspoon vanilla extract
- 2 cups powdered sugar
- 1 teaspoon ground cinnamon

INSTRUCTIONS

1. Preheat the oven to 350 degrees Fahrenheit.

2. To make the bars: In a large bowl, beat the eggs, white sugar, oil, and pumpkin with an electric mixer until light and fluffy. Mix in the flour, baking powder, baking soda, cinnamon, and salt until combined.

3. Spread the batter in an ungreased 10-x-15-inch baking pan. Bake for 20 to 25 minutes, until golden brown and a toothpick inserted into the center comes out clean. Cool completely on a wire rack.

4. For the frosting, in a medium bowl with an electric mixer, cream together the cream cheese, butter, and vanilla until smooth. Gradually add the powdered sugar and cinnamon while mixing. Spread over the cooled bars, then cut into bars.

JULIE'S *Notes*

Store covered in the refrigerator for up to 3 days.

Scan for more tips!

DESSERTS

20 BARS

PREP TIME: 15 MINS

COOK TIME: 5 MINS

COOL TIME: 1 HR

TOTAL TIME: 1 HR 20 MINS

PEANUT BUTTER CEREAL *Bars*

These easy no-bake bars feature Cheerios, Rice Krispies, M&M's, and peanuts. They're perfectly ooey and gooey.

INGREDIENTS

Nonstick cooking spray
4 cups Cheerios cereal
4 cups Rice Krispies cereal
2 cups regular M&M's
2 cups dry-roasted peanuts
2 cups light corn syrup
1¾ cups white granulated sugar
2½ cups creamy peanut butter
1¾ teaspoons vanilla extract

INSTRUCTIONS

1. Lightly spray a 10-x-15-inch pan with nonstick cooking spray.

2. In a large bowl, combine the Cheerios, Rice Krispies, M&M's, and peanuts.

3. In a medium saucepan, bring the corn syrup and sugar to a boil over medium-high heat, stirring frequently. Remove from the heat. Stir in the peanut butter and vanilla.

4. Pour the peanut butter mixture over the cereal mixture in the large bowl. Toss to coat evenly. Spread the mixture evenly in the pan. Let the bars cool until set, about 1 hour, then cut and serve immediately.

JULIE'S *Notes*

Store any leftover bars in an airtight container at room temperature for up to 3 days.

Scan for more tips!

SALTED NUT ROLL *Bars*

This copycat candy bar dessert has a cake batter bottom that is topped with gooey marshmallows, peanuts, and a peanut butter sauce. The bars are soft, chewy, buttery, and oh so good.

SERVES 20

PREP TIME: 10 MINS
COOK TIME: 20 MINS
CHILL TIME: 1 HR
TOTAL TIME: 1 HRS 30 MINS

INGREDIENTS

- Nonstick cooking spray
- 1 (15.25-ounce) box yellow cake mix
- 1 egg
- ¾ cup salted butter, melted, divided
- 3 cups miniature marshmallows
- 1 (10-ounce) package peanut butter chips
- ½ cup corn syrup
- 1 teaspoon vanilla extract
- 2 cups peanuts
- 2 cups Rice Krispies cereal

INSTRUCTIONS

1. Preheat the oven to 350 degrees Fahrenheit. Lightly spray a 9-x-13-inch pan with nonstick cooking spray.
2. In a large bowl, mix the cake mix, egg, and ¼ cup of the melted butter. Spread in the pan and bake for 10 to 12 minutes.
3. Spread the marshmallows on top of the hot crust. Return to the oven and bake for 3 minutes, or until the marshmallows are puffed up.
4. Combine the peanut butter chips, corn syrup, and remaining ½ cup butter in a large saucepan over medium-low heat until melted and combined. Remove from the heat and stir in the vanilla. Then add the peanuts and Rice Krispies and mix well.
5. Pour the peanut sauce over the marshmallows. Refrigerate for about 1 hour, but make sure to cut into bars before it gets too hard.

JULIE'S *Notes*

Store the bars in a covered container at room temperature for up to 3 days.

Scan for more tips!

DESSERTS

20 BARS

PREP TIME: 20 MINS
COOK TIME: 30 MINS
TOTAL TIME: 50 MINS

KNOCK YOU NAKED *Bars*

These are delicious caramel cookie bars with an amazing layer of gooey caramel (with just a hint of peanut butter) stuffed in between cookie layers. You might be wondering why they are called this crazy name. My brother decided they would knock you naked after one bite, and the name was born!

INGREDIENTS

BARS
- Nonstick cooking spray
- 2¼ cups all-purpose flour
- 1 teaspoon baking soda
- 1 teaspoon salt
- 1 cup salted butter, softened
- ¾ cup white granulated sugar
- ¾ cup packed brown sugar
- 1 teaspoon vanilla extract
- 2 eggs
- 2 cups (12 ounces) semi-sweet chocolate chips

CARAMEL SAUCE
- 1 (14-ounce) bag soft caramels, unwrapped
- 1 (5-ounce) can evaporated milk
- ½ cup creamy peanut butter

INSTRUCTIONS

1. Preheat the oven to 375 degrees Fahrenheit. Lightly spray a 9-x-13-inch baking pan with nonstick cooking spray.

2. In a medium bowl, combine the flour, baking soda, and salt.

3. In a large bowl with an electric mixer or in the bowl of a stand mixer, beat the butter, white and brown sugars, and vanilla until creamy. Add the eggs one at a time, beating well after each addition. Gradually mix in the flour mixture. Stir in the chocolate chips.

4. Spread half the cookie dough in the pan. (Set the other half the dough aside.) Bake for 8 to 10 minutes.

5. While the cookie dough is baking, melt the caramels and evaporated milk in a double boiler (see Julie's Notes). Add the peanut butter and thoroughly mix until melted.

6. Spread the caramel sauce over the baked cookie dough base. Drop the remaining cookie dough by spoonfuls on top of the caramel mixture. Bake for 15 to 20 minutes, until the top is light golden brown.

7. Let the bars cool completely. Cut into bars and serve.

JULIE'S *Notes*

If you don't have a double boiler you can make one by putting a heatproof bowl on top of a saucepan. Fill the saucepan with a few inches of cold water, making sure the water doesn't touch the bottom of your bowl. Bring the water to a boil, add the caramels and evaporated milk to the bowl, and stir until the caramels are melted.

Store at room temperature in an airtight container for up to 3 days.

Scan for more tips!

238 JULIE'S EATS & TREATS COOKBOOK

MONSTER COOKIE *Bars*

This quick and easy big batch dessert can be made in less than an hour. The bars taste like your favorite cookie, but are so much easier to make.

PREP TIME: 20 MINS
COOK TIME: 20 MINS
TOTAL TIME: 40 MINS

INGREDIENTS

- Nonstick cooking spray
- ½ cup salted butter, softened
- 1 cup white granulated sugar
- 1 cup packed brown sugar
- 3 eggs, lightly beaten
- 1 teaspoon vanilla extract
- 1 teaspoon corn syrup
- 2 teaspoons baking soda
- 1½ cups creamy peanut butter
- 4½ cups quick rolled oats
- 6 ounces (1 cup) chocolate chips
- 6 ounces M&M's

INSTRUCTIONS

1. Preheat the oven to 350 degrees Fahrenheit. Lightly spray a 13-x-18-inch baking pan with nonstick cooking spray.

2. In a large bowl, beat together the butter and white and brown sugars until they are light and creamy. Add the eggs, vanilla, corn syrup, and baking soda and mix until just combined. Sir in the peanut butter and mix until combined, then stir in the oats.

3. Add the chocolate chips and gently mix by hand until combined. Spread the cookie dough in the prepared pan. Sprinkle the M&M's on top and gently press them into the dough.

4. Bake for 15 minutes for soft, chewy bars. They will not look done, but they will continue to cook as they set. Let the bars cool completely, then cut and serve.

JULIE'S *Notes*

We like to change it up with peanut butter chips and Reese's Pieces instead of chocolate chips and M&M's.

For thicker bars, use a 9-x-13-inch pan and increase the baking time to about 20 minutes.

Store covered at room temperature for up to 3 days.

Scan for more tips!

DESSERTS

16 COOKIES

PREP TIME: 20 MINS
COOK TIME: 10 MINS
TOTAL TIME: 30 MINS

OATMEAL *Cookies*

These soft and chewy oatmeal cookies are the perfect base for all your favorite add-ins—see Julie's Notes.

INGREDIENTS

1 cup salted butter, softened
¾ cup white granulated sugar
1 cup lightly packed brown sugar
2 eggs
2 teaspoons vanilla extract
2 cups all-purpose flour
1 teaspoon baking soda
2 teaspoons ground cinnamon
1 teaspoon ground nutmeg
½ teaspoon salt
3 cups old-fashioned rolled oats

INSTRUCTIONS

1. Preheat the oven to 375 degrees Fahrenheit. Line a large baking sheet with parchment paper.

2. In a large bowl with an electric mixer or in the bowl of a stand mixer, cream together the butter and white and brown sugars until light and fluffy, about 3 minutes. Mix in the eggs one at a time, beating well after each addition. Stir in the vanilla. Stir in the flour, baking soda, cinnamon, nutmeg, and salt. Fold in the oats. If you are using any add-ins (see Julie's Notes), fold them in with the oats.

3. Roll 2-inch portions of the dough (I use a 2-inch cookie scoop for this step) into balls and place on the baking sheet 1½ to 2 inches apart. Gently press each cookie down just slightly with a fork or the palm of your hand.

4. Bake for 8 to 10 minutes, until the edges are golden brown. Let the cookies sit on the pan for 2 minutes before moving to a wire cooling rack.

JULIE'S *Notes*

Add-in ideas include raisins, chocolate chips, dried cranberries, and chopped walnuts or pecans. I recommend ½ to 1 cup of the add-in you choose, but it can vary according to your preference.

Store cookies in an airtight container at room temperature for up to 4 days. To freeze, place in a freezer container or freezer bag and freeze for up to 3 months.

Scan for more tips!

CHOCOLATE CHIP *Cookies*

36 COOKIES

PREP TIME: 15 MINS
COOK TIME: 12 MINS
TOTAL TIME: 27 MINS

Looking for that go-to classic chocolate chip cookie recipe that is no-fail, uses simple ingredients, and doesn't require any chill time? This is the recipe you are going to reach for every single time. I have tested and retested it for years to get it perfect just for you.

INGREDIENTS

- Nonstick cooking spray
- 3 cups all-purpose flour
- 1 teaspoon baking soda
- 1 teaspoon salt
- 1 cup salted butter, softened
- 1½ cups packed brown sugar
- 1 teaspoon vanilla extract
- 2 eggs, room temperature
- 1½ cups (9 ounces) semi-sweet chocolate chips

INSTRUCTIONS

1. Preheat the oven to 350 degrees Fahrenheit. Lightly spray two baking sheets with nonstick cooking spray.
2. In a medium bowl, mix the flour, baking soda, and salt.
3. In a large bowl with an electric mixer or in the bowl of a stand mixer, mix the butter with the brown sugar. Add the vanilla and eggs and mix until it's smooth and fluffy. Add the flour mixture to the wet ingredients and mix to combine. Then stir in the chocolate chips.
4. Drop by spoonfuls onto the baking sheets, 1½ to 2 inches apart, and bake for 10 to 12 minutes, until the bottoms are golden brown.
5. Let sit on the baking sheets for 5 minutes, then remove to a wire rack and let cool.

JULIE'S *Notes*

When the cookies come out of the oven, the tops might still look doughy. But they will continue cooking as they sit on the baking sheet.

Store cookies in an airtight container at room temperature for up to 4 days. To freeze, place in a freezer container or freezer bag and freeze for up to 3 months.

Scan for more tips!

DESSERTS 245

36 COOKIES

PREP TIME: 25 MINS
CHILL TIME: 30 MINS
COOK TIME: 13 MINS
TOTAL TIME: 1 HR 8 MINS

PUMPKIN SNICKERDOODLE *Cookies*

You'll love these little gems. Pillowy-soft pumpkin snickerdoodles are the perfect fall spin on the classic snickerdoodle cookie. Their spiced pumpkin flavor screams fall.

INGREDIENTS

- 3 cups all-purpose flour
- 2 teaspoons pumpkin pie spice
- 2 teaspoons cream of tartar
- 1 teaspoon baking soda
- ½ teaspoon salt
- ½ teaspoon ground cinnamon
- 1 cup unsalted butter, room temperature
- 1 cup white granulated sugar
- ½ cup packed light brown sugar
- 2 eggs, room temperature
- 2 teaspoons vanilla extract
- ½ cup plain pumpkin purée

CINNAMON SUGAR
- ¼ cup white granulated sugar
- 1 teaspoon ground cinnamon

INSTRUCTIONS

1. In a medium bowl, whisk together the flour, pumpkin pie spice, cream of tartar, baking soda, salt, and cinnamon until well combined.

2. In a large bowl, using an electric mixer or a stand mixer, cream together the butter, white sugar, and brown sugar for 1 to 2 minutes, until they're well combined. Mix in the eggs and vanilla, then mix in the pumpkin purée, stopping to scrape down the sides of the bowl as needed.

3. Add the dry ingredients to the wet ingredients and mix until just combined. The dough will be sticky. Cover tightly and chill in the refrigerator for at least 30 minutes, or up to 48 hours (see Julie's Notes).

4. When you're ready to bake, preheat the oven to 350 degrees Fahrenheit. Line two large baking sheets with parchment paper or silicone baking mats.

5. In a small bowl, whisk together the cinnamon sugar ingredients.

6. Scoop up portions of dough with a 2-Tablespoon cookie scoop and roll into balls. Roll each ball in the cinnamon sugar to coat and place on a baking sheet, making sure to leave a little room between each.

7. Bake for 10 to 13 minutes, until the cookies are set. Cool on the baking sheet for a few minutes, then transfer the cookies to a wire rack to cool completely.

JULIE'S *Notes*

We recommend chilling the cookie dough in the 24- to 48-hour range for the best flavor.

Store cookies in an airtight container at room temperature for up to 4 days. To freeze, place in a freezer container or freezer bag and freeze for up to 3 months.

Scan for more tips!

48 COOKIES

REESE'S PIECES PEANUT BUTTER *Cookies*

These soft and chewy cookies are loaded with peanut butter chips and Reese's Pieces. They freeze great and are so delicious.

PREP TIME: 25 MINS

COOK TIME: 11 MINS

TOTAL TIME: 36 MINS

INGREDIENTS

1 cup creamy peanut butter

1 cup salted butter, room temperature, divided

¼ cup honey

3 cups all-purpose flour

1 teaspoon baking powder

½ teaspoon baking soda

½ teaspoon salt

¼ cup butter-flavored shortening

1 cup white granulated sugar

1 cup packed brown sugar

2 eggs

1 teaspoon vanilla extract

1 cup Reese's Pieces

1 cup peanut butter chips

INSTRUCTIONS

1. Preheat the oven to 350 degrees Fahrenheit. Line two large baking sheets with parchment paper or silicone baking mats.

2. In a small bowl, use an electric mixer to mix the peanut butter, ¼ cup of the butter, and the honey.

3. In a medium bowl, mix the flour, baking powder, baking soda, and salt until just combined.

4. In a large bowl, cream the remaining ¾ cup butter, the shortening, and white and brown sugars until light and fluffy. Add the eggs, beating well after each one. Then add the vanilla and reserved peanut butter mixture and mix until just combined.

5. Add the flour mixture to the cookie dough by the cupful and beat at a low speed until the dough is fully mixed. Mix in the Reese's Pieces and peanut butter chips by hand.

6. Drop the dough by spoonfuls onto the cookie sheets about 2 inches apart. Bake for 11 minutes. They won't look quite done, but this short time will keep them soft.

7. Remove from the oven and let them sit on the baking sheet for 1 minute, then transfer to a cooling rack.

JULIE'S *Notes*

Store cookies in an airtight container at room temperature for up to 4 days. To freeze, place in a freezer container or freezer bag and freeze for up to 3 months.

SERVES 16

PREP TIME: 15 MINS
COOK TIME: 30 MINS
TOTAL TIME: 45 MINS

CHOCOLATE CHERRY *Brownies*

I remember my mom making these when I was growing up, and there's just something about that chocolate and cherry combination that is delicious. After baking, drizzle these with cherry pie filling for some extra decadence.

INGREDIENTS

BROWNIES
- Nonstick cooking spray
- 1 (15.25-ounce) package devil's food cake mix
- 1 (21-ounce) can cherry pie filling
- 2 eggs, lightly beaten
- 1 teaspoon almond extract

ICING
- 2 cups white granulated sugar
- ½ cup salted butter
- ½ cup milk
- 1¼ cups (7½ ounces) chocolate chips

INSTRUCTIONS

1. Preheat the oven to 350 degrees Fahrenheit. Grease a 10-x-15-inch jelly roll pan.

2. In a large bowl, mix the cake mix, cherry pie filling, eggs, and almond extract until they are completely combined. Pour into the prepared pan and bake for 20 to 30 minutes, until a toothpick inserted into the middle of the brownies comes out clean.

3. As soon as you take the brownies out of the oven, prepare the icing: In a medium saucepan, bring the sugar, butter, and milk to a boil over medium heat. Boil for 1 minute, then add the chocolate chips. Stir until the chips are melted.

4. Spread the icing on the warm brownies. Let the brownies cool completely and the icing harden before cutting into bars.

JULIE'S *Notes*

Store the brownies in an airtight container at room temperature for 3 to 4 days. To freeze, place in a freezer-safe container and freeze for up to 3 months.

Scan for more tips!

Index

A
Alfredo Bake, Chicken, 141
Apple Crisp, 225
asparagus: Steak, Potatoes, and Asparagus, Sheet Pan, 182

B
bacon
    Bacon Ranch Chicken Sandwiches, Slow Cooker, 142
    Bacon-Wrapped Green Beans, 92
    Breakfast Crescent Ring, 28
    Breakfast Enchiladas, 32
    Cheesy Bacon Ranch Potatoes, 87
    Pea Salad, 67
    Totchos, 158
    Zuppa Toscana, Slow Cooker, 116
Baked Chicken Drumsticks, 122
Baked Chicken Thighs, 125
Baked Chicken Wings, 126
Baked Meatballs in Marinara Sauce, 174
Baked Spaghetti, 149
Baked Sweet and Sour Chicken, 129
Baked Tacos, 161
bananas
    Banana Bars, 230
    Banana Bread, 51
    Banana Chocolate Chip Muffins, 44
bars. see also cookies; desserts
    Banana Bars, 230
    Chocolate Cherry Brownies, 250
    Knock You Naked Bars, 238
    Monster Cookie Bars, 241
    Peanut Butter Cereal Bars, 234
    Pumpkin Bars, 233
    Rice Krispie Treats, The Best, 213
    Salted Nut Roll Bars, 237
beans
    Baked Tacos, 161
    Burrito Bowl, One-Pot, 166
    Chili, 111
    Enchilada Soup, Slow Cooker, 115
    Totchos, 158
    White Chicken Chili, Slow Cooker, 112
beef
    Beef and Broccoli, 177
    Beef Stew, Slow Cooker, 119
    French Dip Sandwiches, Slow Cooker, 185
    Garlic-Butter Steak and Potatoes, 181
    Mississippi Pot Roast, Slow Cooker, 186
    Steak, Potatoes, and Asparagus, Sheet Pan, 182

beef, ground
    Baked Meatballs in Marinara Sauce, 174
    Baked Spaghetti, 149
    Baked Tacos, 161
    Beef Enchiladas, 162
    Burrito Bowl, One-Pot, 166
    Chili, 111
    Dorito Taco Salad, 72
    Hamburger and Wild Rice Casserole, Slow Cooker, 154
    Hamburger Soup, 104
    Hamburger Stroganoff, 170
    Lasagna, 178
    Lasagna Soup, 108
    Mini Meatloaves, 157
    Stuffed Pepper Casserole, 173
    Taco Pasta, One-Pot, 165
    Taco Pie, 169
    Zucchini Hamburger Skillet, 153
Beer Bread, 56
bell peppers
    Chicken Fajitas, Sheet Pan, 134
    Stuffed Pepper Casserole, 173
Berry Baked Oatmeal, 20
The Best Rice Krispie Treats, 213
Biscuit and Gravy Breakfast Casserole, 36
Biscuits, Cheddar, 59
blackberries: Fruit Pizza, 229
blueberries
    Blueberry Muffins, 46
    Fruit Pizza, 229
Boats, Stuffed Zucchini, 189
Boil, Shrimp, 201
breads. see also muffins
    Banana Bread, 51
    Beer Bread, 56
    Cheddar Biscuits, 59
    Cheesy Garlic Bread, 55
    Pumpkin Bread, 52
    Texas Roadhouse Rolls, 60–61
breakfasts. see also breads; muffins
    Casserole, Biscuit and Gravy Breakfast, 36
    Casserole, Hash Brown Breakfast, 35
    Cinnamon Rolls, Easy, 38–39
    Crescent Ring, Breakfast, 28
    Enchiladas, Breakfast, 32
    French Toast, 27
    Ham and Cheese Egg Muffins, 31
    Oatmeal, Berry Baked, 20
    Pancakes, Fluffy, 23
    Waffles, 24

Broccoli, Beef and, 177
Broccoli Cheese Soup, 96
Brownies, Chocolate Cherry, 250
Brussels sprouts: Oven-Roasted Vegetables, 91
Bundt Cake, Lemon, 217
Burrito Bowl, One-Pot, 166
Buster Bar Dessert, 210

C
Cajun Chicken Pasta, One-Pot, 146
cake mix, boxed
    Chocolate Cherry Brownies, 250
    Lemon Bundt Cake, 217
    Oreo Poke Cake, 221
    Salted Nut Roll Bars, 237
    Strawberry Poke Cake, 218
cakes. see also desserts
    Cheesecake, No-Bake, 214
    Lemon Bundt Cake, 217
    Oreo Poke Cake, 221
    Strawberry Poke Cake, 218
Caramel Sauce (under Knock You Naked Bars), 238
carrots
    Beef Stew, Slow Cooker, 119
    Broccoli Cheese Soup, 96
    Chicken and Rice Soup, 99
    Creamy Chicken Noodle Soup, 100
    Oven-Roasted Vegetables, 91
    Sausage and Potato Soup, 107
casseroles and pasta bakes
    Chicken Alfredo Bake, 141
    Chicken Tetrazzini, 138
    Ham and Potato Casserole, 194
    Hamburger and Wild Rice Casserole, Slow Cooker, 154
    Hash Brown Breakfast Casserole, 35
    Stuffed Pepper Casserole, 173
Catalina dressing: Dorito Taco Salad, 72
Cereal Bars, Peanut Butter, 234
cheddar
    Bacon Ranch Chicken Sandwiches, Slow Cooker, 142
    Beef Enchiladas, 162
    Breakfast Crescent Ring, 28
    Breakfast Enchiladas, 32
    Broccoli Cheese Soup, 96
    Cheddar Biscuits, 59
    Cheesy Bacon Ranch Potatoes, 87
    Cheesy Garlic Bread, 55
    Creamy Chicken Enchiladas, 137

Dorito Taco Salad, 72
Funeral Potatoes, 88
Ham and Cheese Egg Muffins, 31
Hash Brown Breakfast Casserole, 35
Homemade Hamburger Helper, 150
Macaroni Salad, 71
Mini Meatloaves, 157
Pea Salad, 67
Sausage and Potato Soup, 107
Stuffed Pepper Casserole, 173
Taco Pasta, One-Pot, 165
Taco Pie, 169
Totchos, 158
Cheerios: Peanut Butter Cereal Bars, 234
cheese. *see specific cheeses*
Cheesecake, No-Bake, 214
Cheesy Garlic Bread, 55
Cheesy Garlic-Butter Pasta, 83
cherry pie filling
Chocolate Cherry Brownies, 250
No-Bake Cheesecake, 214
chicken
Bacon Ranch Chicken Sandwiches,
Slow Cooker, 142
Baked Chicken Drumsticks, 122
Baked Chicken Thighs, 125
Baked Chicken Wings, 126
Baked Sweet and Sour Chicken, 129
Cajun Chicken Pasta, One-Pot, 146
Chicken Alfredo Bake, 141
Chicken and Rice Soup, 99
Chicken and Wild Rice Soup, 103
Chicken Fajitas, Sheet Pan, 134
Chicken Fried Rice, 133
Chicken Tetrazzini, 138
Creamy Chicken Enchiladas, 137
Creamy Chicken Noodle Soup, 100
Enchilada Soup, Slow Cooker, 115
Honey Sesame Chicken, 130
Italian Chicken, Slow Cooker, 145
White Chicken Chili, Slow Cooker, 112
Chili, 111
Chili, White Chicken, Slow Cooker, 112
chips, nacho cheese: Taco Pie, 169
chocolate, 209
Banana Chocolate Chip Muffins, 44
Buster Bar Dessert, 210
Chocolate Cherry Brownies, 250
Chocolate Chip Cookies, 245
Hot Fudge Sauce, 206
Knock You Naked Bars, 238
Monster Cookie Bars, 241
Oreo Poke Cake, 221
Peanut Butter Cereal Bars, 234
cinnamon
Apple Crisp, 225
Cinnamon Rolls, Easy, 38–39
Cruffins, 48

Pumpkin Bars, 233
Pumpkin Snickerdoodle Cookies,
246–247
Colby jack
Ham and Potato Casserole, 194
Zucchini Hamburger Skillet, 153
cookies. *see also* bars
Chocolate Chip Cookies, 245
Monster Cookie Bars, 241
Oatmeal Cookies, 242
Pumpkin Snickerdoodle Cookies,
246–247
Reese's Pieces Peanut Butter Cookies,
249
Sugar Cookie Crust (under Fruit Pizza),
229
Cool Whip
Oreo Fluff, 75
Oreo Poke Cake, 221
Strawberry Poke Cake, 218
Strawberry Pretzel Salad, 76
corn
Burrito Bowl, One-Pot, 166
Enchilada Soup, Slow Cooker, 115
Hamburger Soup, 104
Shrimp Boil, 201
Totchos, 158
White Chicken Chili, Slow Cooker, 112
cornflakes: Funeral Potatoes, 88
cottage cheese
Baked Spaghetti, 149
Lasagna, 178
cream cheese
Bacon Ranch Chicken Sandwiches,
Slow Cooker, 142
Banana Bars, 230
Cinnamon Rolls, Easy, 38–39
Cream Cheese Frosting (under Easy
Cinnamon Rolls), 38–39
Fruit Pizza, 229
Italian Chicken, Slow Cooker, 145
No-Bake Cheesecake, 214
Pumpkin Bars, 233
Strawberry Pretzel Salad, 76
Creamy Chicken Enchiladas, 137
Creamy Chicken Noodle Soup, 100
crescent rolls
Breakfast Crescent Ring, 28
Cruffins, 48
Taco Pie, 169
Crisp, Apple, 225
Crisp, Strawberry, 222
Cruffins, 48

D

desserts. *see also* bars; cakes; cookies
Buster Bar Dessert, 210
Crisp, Apple, 225

Crisp, Strawberry, 222
Fruit Pizza, 229
Hot Fudge Sauce, 206
Oreo Fluff, 75
Oreo Ice Cream Dessert, 209
Strawberry Pie, 226
Strawberry Pretzel Salad, 76
Dorito Taco Salad, 72
Dressing, Homemade Italian, 64
Drumsticks, Baked Chicken, 122

E

eggs
Biscuit and Gravy Breakfast Casserole,
36
Breakfast Crescent Ring, 28
Breakfast Enchiladas, 32
Ham and Cheese Egg Muffins, 31
Hash Brown Breakfast Casserole, 35
Potato Bake, 68
Enchiladas, Beef, 162
Enchiladas, Breakfast, 32
Enchiladas, Creamy Chicken, 137
Enchilada Soup, Slow Cooker, 115

F

Fajitas, Sheet Pan Chicken, 134
Fish: Parmesan-Crusted Tilapia, 198
Fluff, Oreo, 75
Fluffy Pancakes, 23
French Dip Sandwiches, Slow Cooker,
185
French onion soup mix: Mississippi Pot
Roast, Slow Cooker, 186
French Toast, 27
Fried Rice, 79
Fried Rice, Chicken, 133
frostings and icings
under Banana Bars, 230
under Chocolate Cherry
Brownies, 250
Cream Cheese Frosting (under Easy
Cinnamon Rolls), 38–39
under Pumpkin Bars, 333
Fruit Pizza, 229
Funeral Potatoes, 88

G

garlic
Cheesy Garlic Bread, 55
Cheesy Garlic-Butter Pasta, 83
Garlic-Butter Steak and Potatoes, 181
graham cracker crumbs: No-Bake
Cheesecake, 214
Gravy, Biscuit and, Breakfast Casserole, 36
green beans
Bacon-Wrapped Green Beans, 92
Hamburger Soup, 104

green chiles
  Beef Enchiladas, 162
  Burrito Bowl, One-Pot, 166
  Creamy Chicken Enchiladas, 137
  Enchilada Soup, Slow Cooker, 115
  White Chicken Chili, Slow Cooker, 112
grocery lists, 15

H

ham
  Ham and Cheese Egg Muffins, 31
  Ham and Potato Casserole, 194
  Hash Brown Breakfast Casserole, 35
  Macaroni Salad, 71
Hamburger Helper, Homemade, 150
Hamburger Soup, 104
Hamburger Stroganoff, 170
hash browns
  Funeral Potatoes, 88
  Hash Brown Breakfast Casserole, 35
Honey Sesame Chicken, 130
Hot Fudge Sauce, 206
  in Oreo Ice Cream Dessert, 209

I

ice cream
  Buster Bar Dessert, 210
  Oreo Ice Cream Dessert, 209
Italian Chicken, Slow Cooker, 145
Italian Dressing, Homemade, 64
Italian dressing mix: Italian Chicken, Slow
  Cooker, 145

J

Jell-O
  Strawberry Pie, 226
  Strawberry Poke Cake, 218
  Strawberry Pretzel Salad, 76

K

kale: Zuppa Toscana, Slow Cooker, 116
kids in the kitchen, 13, 14, 15
kiwis: Fruit Pizza, 229
Knock You Naked Bars, 238

L

Lasagna, 178
Lasagna Soup, 108
Lemon Bundt Cake, 217

M

M&M's
  Bars, Monster Cookie, 241
  Peanut Butter Cereal Bars, 234
Macaroni Salad, 71
marinara sauce
  Baked Meatballs in Marinara Sauce, 174
  Baked Spaghetti, 149

Lasagna Soup, 108
  Pizza Sliders, 190
  Stuffed Zucchini Boats, 189
marshmallows
  Rice Krispie Treats, The Best, 213
  Salted Nut Roll Bars, 237
meal planning, 12
Meatballs in Marinara Sauce, Baked, 174
Meatloaves, Mini, 157
Mexican cheese, shredded
  Baked Tacos, 161
  Burrito Bowl, One-Pot, 166
  Enchilada Soup, Slow Cooker, 115
Mini Meatloaves, 157
Mississippi Pot Roast, Slow Cooker, 186
Monster Cookie Bars, 241
mozzarella
  Baked Meatballs in Marinara Sauce, 174
  Baked Spaghetti, 149
  Cheesy Garlic Bread, 55
  Cheesy Garlic-Butter Pasta, 83
  Chicken Alfredo Bake, 141
  Chicken Tetrazzini, 138
  Lasagna, 178
  Lasagna Soup, 108
  Pizza Pasta, One-Pot, 193
  Pizza Sliders, 190
  Stuffed Zucchini Boats, 189
muffins. see also breads
  Banana Chocolate Chip Muffins, 44
  Blueberry Muffins, 46
  Cruffins, 48
  Ham and Cheese Egg Muffins, 31
mushrooms
  Chicken and Wild Rice Soup, 103
  Hamburger and Wild Rice Casserole,
    Slow Cooker, 154
  Hamburger Stroganoff, 170

N

nacho cheese chips: Taco Pie, 169
nacho cheese sauce: Totchos, 158
No-Bake Cheesecake, 214
Nut Roll Bars, Salted, 237

O

oats and oatmeal
  Apple Crisp, 225
  Berry Baked Oatmeal, 20
  Mini Meatloaves, 157
  Monster Cookie Bars, 241
  Oatmeal Cookies, 242
  Strawberry Crisp, 222
olives: Tossed Salad with Italian Dressing, 64
One-Pot Burrito Bowl, 166
One-Pot Cajun Chicken Pasta, 146
One-Pot Pizza Pasta, 193
One-Pot Taco Pasta, 165

oranges, mandarin: Fruit Pizza, 229
Oreo cookies
  Buster Bar Dessert, 210
  Oreo Fluff, 75
  Oreo Ice Cream Dessert, 209
  Oreo Poke Cake, 221
Oven-Roasted Vegetables, 91

P

Pancakes, Fluffy, 23
pantry staples, 16
parmesan
  Baked Meatballs in Marinara Sauce, 174
  Cajun Chicken Pasta, One-Pot, 146
  Chicken Alfredo Bake, 141
  Lasagna, 178
  Parmesan-Crusted Pork Chops, 197
  Parmesan-Crusted Tilapia, 198
  Pizza Sliders, 190
  Steak, Potatoes, and Asparagus, Sheet
    Pan, 182
  Tossed Salad with Italian Dressing, 64
pasta and noodles
  Alfredo Bake, Chicken, 141
  Cajun Chicken Pasta, One-Pot, 146
  Cheesy Garlic-Butter Pasta, 83
  Chicken Noodle Soup, Creamy, 100
  Hamburger Helper, Homemade, 150
  Lasagna, 178
  Lasagna Soup, 108
  Macaroni Salad, 71
  Pizza Pasta, One-Pot, 193
  Shrimp Pasta, 202
  Spaghetti, Baked, 149
  Stroganoff, Hamburger, 170
  Taco Pasta, One-Pot, 165
  Tetrazzini, Chicken, 138
peanuts and peanut butter
  Buster Bar Dessert, 210
  Knock You Naked Bars, 238
  Monster Cookie Bars, 241
  Peanut Butter Cereal Bars, 234
  Reese's Pieces Peanut Butter Cookies,
    249
  Salted Nut Roll Bars, 237
peas
  Chicken Fried Rice, 133
  Chicken Tetrazzini, 138
  Fried Rice, 79
  Macaroni Salad, 71
  Pea Salad, 67
pepperoncini peppers
  Mississippi Pot Roast, Slow Cooker, 186
  Tossed Salad with Italian Dressing, 64
pepperoni
  Pizza Pasta, One-Pot, 193
  Pizza Sliders, 190
Pie, Strawberry, 226

Pie, Taco, 169
Pizza, Fruit, 229
Pizza Pasta, One-Pot, 193
Pizza Sliders, 190
Poke Cake, Oreo, 221
Poke Cake, Strawberry, 218
Pork Chops, Parmesan-Crusted, 197
potatoes
    Beef Stew, Slow Cooker, 119
    Cheesy Bacon Ranch Potatoes, 87
    Funeral Potatoes, 88
    Garlic-Butter Steak and Potatoes, 181
    Ham and Potato Casserole, 194
    Hamburger Soup, 104
    Hash Brown Breakfast Casserole, 35
    Oven-Roasted Vegetables, 91
    Potato Salad, 68
    Roasted Sweet Potatoes, 84
    Sausage and Potato Soup, 107
    Shrimp Boil, 201
    Steak, Potatoes, and Asparagus, Sheet Pan, 182
    Totchos, 158
    Zuppa Toscana, Slow Cooker, 116
Pot Roast, Mississippi, Slow Cooker, 186
Pretzel Salad, Strawberry, 76
provolone: French Dip Sandwiches, Slow Cooker, 185
pudding, instant
    Oreo Fluff, 75
    Oreo Poke Cake, 221
    Strawberry Poke Cake, 218
pumpkin
    Pumpkin Bars, 233
    Pumpkin Bread, 52
    Pumpkin Snickerdoodle Cookies, 246–247

R

radicchio: Tossed Salad with Italian Dressing, 64
ranch seasoning and dressing
    Bacon Ranch Chicken Sandwiches, Slow Cooker, 142
    Cheesy Bacon Ranch Potatoes, 87
    Mississippi Pot Roast, Slow Cooker, 186
raspberries: Fruit Pizza, 229
Reese's Pieces Peanut Butter Cookies, 249
rice
    Burrito Bowl, One-Pot, 166
    Chicken and Rice Soup, 99
    Chicken and Wild Rice Soup, 103
    Chicken Fried Rice, 133
    Fried Rice, 79
    Hamburger and Wild Rice Casserole, Slow Cooker, 154
    Spanish Rice, 80
    Zucchini Hamburger Skillet, 153

Rice Krispies
    Peanut Butter Cereal Bars, 234
    Rice Krispie Treats, The Best, 213
    Salted Nut Roll Bars, 237
Roasted Sweet Potatoes, 84
Rolls, Texas Roadhouse, 60–61

S

salads
    Dorito Taco Salad, 72
    Macaroni Salad, 71
    Oreo Fluff, 75
    Pea Salad, 67
    Potato Salad, 68
    Strawberry Pretzel Salad, 76
    Tossed Salad with Italian Dressing, 64
salsa
    Baked Tacos, 161
    Burrito Bowl, One-Pot, 166
    Spanish Rice, 80
Salted Nut Roll Bars, 237
sandwiches
    Bacon Ranch Chicken Sandwiches, Slow Cooker, 142
    French Dip Sandwiches, Slow Cooker, 185
    Pizza Sliders, 190
sauces
    Alfredo Sauce (under Chicken Alfredo Bake), 141
    Caramel Sauce (under Knock You Naked Bars), 238
    Honey Sauce (under Honey Sesame Chicken), 130
    Hot Fudge Sauce, 206
    Stir-Fry Sauce (under Beef and Broccoli), 177
sausage
    Biscuit and Gravy Breakfast Casserole, 36
    Breakfast Enchiladas, 32
    Sausage and Potato Soup, 107
    Shrimp Boil, 201
    Stuffed Zucchini Boats, 189
    Zuppa Toscana, Slow Cooker, 116
seafood
    Parmesan-Crusted Tilapia, 198
    Shrimp Boil, 201
    Shrimp Pasta, 202
Sesame Honey Chicken, 130
Sheet Pan Chicken Fajitas, 134
Sheet Pan Steak, Potatoes, and Asparagus, 182
shrimp
    Shrimp Boil, 201
    Shrimp Pasta, 202
sides. see also salads
    Green Beans, Bacon-Wrapped, 92
    Pasta, Cheesy Garlic-Butter, 83

Potatoes, Cheesy Bacon Ranch, 87
Potatoes, Funeral, 88
Rice, Fried, 79
Rice, Spanish, 80
Sweet Potatoes, Roasted, 84
Vegetables, Oven-Roasted, 91
Sliders, Pizza, 190
slow cooker recipes
    Bacon Ranch Chicken Sandwiches, Slow Cooker, 142
    Beef Stew, Slow Cooker, 119
    Enchilada Soup, Slow Cooker, 115
    French Dip Sandwiches, Slow Cooker, 185
    Hamburger and Wild Rice Casserole, Slow Cooker, 154
    Italian Chicken, Slow Cooker, 145
    Mississippi Pot Roast, Slow Cooker, 186
    White Chicken Chili, Slow Cooker, 112
    Zuppa Toscana, Slow Cooker, 116
Snickerdoodle Cookies, Pumpkin, 246–247
soups and stews
    Beef Stew, Slow Cooker, 119
    Broccoli Cheese Soup, 96
    Chicken and Rice Soup, 99
    Chicken and Wild Rice Soup, 103
    Chicken Noodle Soup, Creamy, 100
    Chili, 111
    Chili, White Chicken, Slow Cooker, 112
    Enchilada Soup, Slow Cooker, 115
    Hamburger Soup, 104
    Lasagna Soup, 108
    Sausage and Potato Soup, 107
    Zuppa Toscana, Slow Cooker, 116
Spaghetti, Baked, 149
Spanish Rice, 80
staples, pantry, 16
Steak, Potatoes, and Asparagus, Sheet Pan, 182
Steak and Potatoes, Garlic-Butter, 181
stews. see soups and stews
Stir-Fry Sauce (under Beef and Broccoli), 177
strawberries
    Fruit Pizza, 229
    Strawberry Crisp, 222
    Strawberry Pie, 226
    Strawberry Poke Cake, 218
    Strawberry Pretzel Salad, 76
Stroganoff, Hamburger, 170
Stuffed Pepper Casserole, 173
Stuffed Zucchini Boats, 189
Sweet and Sour Chicken, Baked, 129
sweet potatoes
    Oven-Roasted Vegetables, 91
    Roasted Sweet Potatoes, 84

INDEX   255

T

Taco Pasta, One-Pot, 165
Taco Pie, 169
Tacos, Baked, 161
Taco Salad, Dorito, 72
Tater Tots: Totchos, 158
Tetrazzini, Chicken, 138
Texas Roadhouse Rolls, 60–61
Thighs, Baked Chicken, 125
Tilapia, Parmesan-Crusted, 198
tomatoes
    Dorito Taco Salad, 72
    Shrimp Pasta, 202
    Tossed Salad with Italian Dressing, 64
    Totchos, 158
    Zucchini Hamburger Skillet, 153
tomatoes, canned. *see also* marinara sauce
    Beef Stew, Slow Cooker, 119
    Burrito Bowl, One-Pot, 166
    Chili, 111
    Enchilada Soup, Slow Cooker, 115
    Hamburger Soup, 104
    Lasagna, 178
    Lasagna Soup, 108
    Pizza Pasta, One-Pot, 193
    Stuffed Pepper Casserole, 173
    Taco Pasta, One-Pot, 165
tools, kitchen, 14
tortilla chips, nacho cheese: Taco Pie, 169
Tossed Salad with Italian Dressing, 64
Totchos, 158

V

Vegetables, Oven-Roasted, 91
Velveeta: Taco Pasta, One-Pot, 165

W

Waffles, 24
Wings, Baked Chicken, 126

Z

zucchini
    Oven-Roasted Vegetables, 91
    Stuffed Zucchini Boats, 189
    Zucchini Hamburger Skillet, 153
Zuppa Toscana, Slow Cooker, 116

Copyright © 2024 by Julie Evink, Julie's Eats & Treats, Inc.

All rights reserved. No part of this publication may be reprinted, reproduced, transmitted, or utilized in any form or by any electronic, mechanical, or other means, now known or hereafter invented, including photocopying, microfilming, and recording, or in any information retrieval system without the written permission of Julie, Evink, Julie's Eats & Treats, Inc. For inquiries regarding permissions, translations, foreign rights, audio rights, and any other forms of reproduction, please contact the publisher at www.julieseatsandtreats.com/contact.

Trademark Notice: Product or corporate names may be trademarks or registered trademarks, and are used only for identification and explanation without intent to infringe.

ISBN: 979-8-9895959-0-7

Printed in China

Design by Weller Smith Design, LLC
Lifestyle Photography by Rachel Marthaler
Food Photography by Rebecca Abbott, Natalie Booras, Lindsay Evers, Julie Evink, Carey Gabrielson, Elaine Holli, Sue Kvale, Liz Latham, Allison Miller, Ali Rae, Dasha Rasulova, Sergei Rasulov, Ivy Thurber, Melissa Wilbur

10 9 8 7 6 5 4 3 2 1

First Edition

Published by Julie Evink, Julie's Eats & Treats, Inc.

www.julieseatsandtreats.com